DON GIOVANNI

Parallax Re-visions of Culture and Society

Stephen G. Nichols, Gerald Prince, and Wendy Steiner,
Series Editors

DON GIOVANNI
Myths of Seduction and Betrayal

◉◈◉◈◉◈◉◈◉◈◉◈◉

Edited by
JONATHAN MILLER

The Johns Hopkins University Press
Baltimore

This work was originally published in Great Britain as *The Don Giovanni Book: Myths of Seduction and Betrayal* by Faber and Faber Limited, London. The First American Edition was published by Schocken Books, Inc. and distributed by Pantheon Books, a division of Random House Books, Inc., New York. This Johns Hopkins Paperbacks edition, 1991, is published by arrangement with Schocken Books.

The Johns Hopkins University Press
701 West 40th Street
Baltimore, Maryland 21211-2190

The paper used in this book meets the minimum requirements of American National Standard for Information Sciences—Permanence of Paper for Printed Library Materials, ANSI Z39.48-1984.

Library of Congress Cataloging-in-Publication Data

Don Giovanni: myths of seduction and betrayal / edited by
Jonathan Miller.
p.   cm. — (Parallax)
Reprint. Previously published: New York: Schocken Books, 1990.
Includes bibliographical references.
ISBN 0-8018-4332-4 (pbk.: alk. paper)
1. Don Juan (Legendary character) in literature. 2. Seduction in
literature. 3. Seduction—Social aspects—Europe. I. Miller,
Jonathan, 1934–   . II. Series: Parallax (Baltimore, Md.)
[PN57.D7D59   1991]
809'. 93351—dc20   91-21097

Contents

Introduction

JONATHAN MILLER

Associated with the widely held belief that it is the greatest of
Mozart's operas, *Don Giovanni* has the reputation of being
peculiarly difficult to stage. What makes a piece of theatre
'difficult to stage'? *King Lear*, for instance, was considered
unperformable by Dr Johnson. Certainly, the unspeakable
horror of watching Gloucester's eyes put out, or the cruel
humiliation of Lear, make the play a painful experience. Yet the
option exists to enjoy it as literature just by reading it, without
actually seeing it on the stage.

But unlike a play whose dramatic virtues can be recognized on
the page – and just as often disperse on the stage – the quality of
an opera is not readily detectable until it *has* been performed. An
unperformed opera is literally a closed book to all but a very few
musicians who can visualize the action and hear the music from
the score alone.

So, unless one agrees with the self-defeating claim that the
greatness of *Don Giovanni* is contained *within* the music, so that
it does not need to be seen, it is difficult to see how the opera's
reputation for greatness could have been achieved without at least
one satisfactory performance. Even if 'greatness' has a useful
meaning, which I doubt, it is merely sentimental to insist that
certain works are 'too subtle', 'too majestic' – 'too great' – for
mere mortals to reproduce them.

Nevertheless, *Don Giovanni* does present quite special
problems in performance, problems which, by no coincidence,
arise from the mythological quality of the work, from its deep

roots in an emotional experience – conscious and unconscious – that we all share, and which is precisely, perhaps, what leads us to call this opera 'great'.

To begin with, what *sort* of work is *Don Giovanni*? With its perplexing alternations of farce and ferocity, natural comedy and gothic horror, it is notoriously hard to achieve dramatic consistency. The producer is often left with the paralysing conviction that he has failed to identify the framework within which these discrepancies of tone might otherwise be reconciled.

And beyond the structural ambiguity there is then the inescapable ambiguity of every aspect of the opera's foreground: time, space and character. In *Figaro* and *Così* there are reassuring unities of time and space and, because the scenes succeed one another intelligibly, the producer is never left with the suspicion that the action is dispersing as he rehearses it. In *Don Giovanni*, although most of the action seems to occur in the open air, it is impossible to tell how any one street scene is related to any other. And just when we think we can be sure that the characters are indoors, interiors and exteriors seem to blend. In what sort of labyrinth, for example, does the second-act sextet take place? Where is Elvira looking for an exit, and where Leporello? And again, without anything to explain the transition, the scene where the disguised trio arrives in front of Don Giovanni's palace dissolves into the revel. Throughout the opera the characters wander, as though in a nightmare, through apparently familiar locations – a dishevelled landscape in which places which ought to be separate from one another are mysteriously adjacent.

The uncertainty of time and space is echoed by a comparable indeterminacy of character. Who *are* these people? Titles define the roles (Donna Anna, Commendatore, etc.) yet we never see the settings which would assign a social reality to them. Restless and unhoused, they project passions without displaying anything one would wish to call a *personality*. In *The Marriage of Figaro* we would never question the social position of Almaviva, whom we see in daylight for three acts, in his own house surrounded by the social courtesies of his world and bounded by the understandable restraints which it imposes. But Don Giovanni keeps no household, merely a derelict establishment with a posse of musicians. Even in *Così*, when relationships are deliberately flattened and diagrammatic, the domestic framework visibly stabilizes the identity of the six artificial characters.

In *Don Giovanni*, the absence of a social setting makes it notoriously hard for the singers to 'centre' their performances. We are never allowed to see them in anything as recognizable as a house, so they tend to dematerialize, and it is only too easy to portray them as demented banshees weightlessly haunting an abandoned city.

But that may be the point. Perhaps it is altogether wrong to seek the traditional co-ordinates of dramatic action. Perhaps by trying to make the roles conform to the accepted canons of character and personality one is forcing them to assume an identity which is inconsistent with the essence of this opera. In fact, if one does not resist the chaotic turbulence within which the characters swirl like human debris, and if, like Poe's sailor, one submits to its spiralling momentum, the action and characterization take care of themselves. Everyone is swept towards the irresistible vortex of the opera's conclusion.

In rehearsal I have found this to be the only available strategy. It seems that there is, after all, something to be said for the argument that the drama of *Don Giovanni* is exposed in the music (though it is difficult to convince professional performers that any attempt to visualize social reality is doomed to failure – that nothing is to be gained by trying to find a foothold on the polished slopes of Mozart's maelstrom). Nevertheless, if the work is to be staged at all, one cannot expect the audience to follow Kierkegaard's example, and face the back wall. The opera must be made visible. A foothold must somehow be found by the producer.

In preparing the English National Opera production which was the occasion of this book, a number of ideas emerged which are reflected in the nine essays collected here. The authors of these pieces, each writing from within different disciplines, have illuminated aspects of the opera's dramatic substance. Although it is self-defeating to introduce conventional questions of motivation, each performer in the opera has to *do* something and *be* someone. The visible actions, such as they are, have also to be explained and justified. They have to be set within a frame of reference that makes some sort of sense. While the discussions of our nine contributors are exhilaratingly varied, all tackle the opera's wider reference, from the seventeenth century of Don Giovanni's pre-operatic birth, to his significance in our post-Freudian twentieth century.

For there is no escape from the fact that the main characters have a conspicuous existence outside the opera. The problematical aloofness from the hard realities of time, space and character may worry performers and producers, but it allows Mozart and da Ponte to preserve the mythological quality of their characters. They arrive on the operatic stage with a reputation which has grown elsewhere and, in the case of the title role, with something of the awkward unmanageability of a visiting celebrity. Peter Conrad, in 'The Libertine's Progress' (p. 81), has sketched this celebrity's biography, describing him as 'the man of the senses who intends both to know and to own everything, and whose mode of doing so is to make love'. Conrad compares Don Giovanni to Faust – 'the man of the mind who wants to know everything'.

The comparison is useful. Faust is indeed another figure whose personality is overwhelmed by the shadows cast by his alternative incarnations. But the likeness goes deeper. If *Don Giovanni* can be said to be *about* anything, it is, among other things, about the dangers of over-reaching. Faust loses his soul by impudently using it to purchase omniscience. Don Giovanni spends *his* soul trying to assert sexual omnipotence. Both characters come to grief by failing to recognize that human powers are bounded and that the identifiability of an individual personality is annihilated by the attempt to include everything.

In analytic terms, therefore, one can visualize Faust, and especially Don Giovanni, as failures of the maturational process, that is to say, of the process by which the developing infant sees and eventually settles for the unsurpassable difference between self and non-self. Thus, in the cognitive sphere for example, there are limits to what is knowable, and the ambition to understand and control the whole of nature is inconsistent with being the sort of thing that human beings are. And the same applies to the domain of desire. The attempt to conquer and assimilate the bodies of 2,064 others is the result of failing to recognize the separate emotional existence of even one.

Peter Gay, in 'The Father's Revenge' (p. 70), offers a similar analysis in his Freudian account of *Don Giovanni*. 'His restless inability to find lasting gratification with anyone . . . suggests an unresolved Oedipal fixation . . . The Don knows in his heart that each new conquest must fail him.' Apart from the fact that it leaves a trail of emotional destruction, a career of such narcissistic exorbitance consumes its protagonist. Desire renews itself with each climax: no sooner has he overcome the tyranny of one pursuit than he is overwhelmed by the tumescence aroused by the next. Far from going to hell at the conclusion of the opera he is in it from the start. And, if the work is to have any emotional reality at all, the performer must let the audience see the famished exhaustion of his existence, and that the willingness with which he undertakes to entertain the stone visitor reflects a growing realization that death is perhaps the only sanctuary in which such a morbidly insatiable self can find its peace.

Which brings up the question of how to visualize the descent into hell. Sanctuary though it might be, Mozart and da Ponte also meant it to be seen as a place of penal custody. Since modern audiences find devils laughable, 'an outmoded moral relic' as Lawrence Lipking puts it in his contribution 'Donna Abbandonata' (p. 36), it is necessary to find some alternatives to act as agents of the Don's arrest. We no longer see hell in terms of some physical punishment or as a geographical location. We have more subtle and sophisticated views: Graham Greene, for instance, would say that hell is a sense of loss at being at a distance from God's love; Sartre that 'hell is other people'. Professor Lipking suggests that the role of Donna Elvira implies another kind of hell for Don Giovanni: the isolation he brings upon himself. 'I myself am hell; nobody's here.'

In the ENO production, it was indeed the women abandoned

by Don Giovanni who loomed out of the darkness as the obvious instruments of his doom, an idea I had after reading Richard Cobb's account, in *Death in Paris*, of the women found drowned in the Seine in the eighteenth century. At that time, women who fell from the position of honourable chastity and who failed to have their sexual conquest subsequently sanctified by marriage, sank into a sort of death in life – a limbo of exclusion from society, of dishonour and disgrace that very often led to suicide.

In the light of such evidence, it is difficult for Leporello to perform the catalogue aria in the usual mood of unbridled merriment. In rehearsing the scene with Elvira, the knowledge that such a long list of amorous conquests implied a short, or perhaps not so short, appendix of tragedies and even suicides, led us to sadden the end of the song, as if Leporello becomes infected by Elvira's despondency and sees, perhaps for the first time, that he has been the unwitting but nonetheless culpable assistant of a truly deplorable enterprise: he has reasons for leaving the Don's service over and above the risks of vengeance. In any case there is much more at stake than either vengeance or conscience. As the accomplice of his master's pleasure, Leporello surrenders any claims he might have had to a sexual identity of his own and, as we can tell from the aria with which he opens the opera, he is condemned to await the conclusion of someone else's delight. Robert Darnton's story (p. 20) of a real-life Don Juan in eighteenth-century France, 'Don Juanism from Below', well conveys this hellish hidden aspect of the rake's progress.

It is not difficult to visualize the dank morgues in which so many of the despairing victims of the Don's delight yielded up their post-mortem secrets. Indeed, the ambience which created Leporello's catalogue, also led to the first post-mortem statistics. Autopsies were carried out as part of a systematic attempt to correlate the symptoms of disease with the appearance of various organs after death. Such an interest inevitably extended to include social as well as biological causes of death. As Cobb shows, the contents of a dead man's pockets can be just as eloquent as the post-mortem appearance of heart and spleen. The fascinating association between the first replicas of post-mortems – the wax models of Zummo – and the species of funerary sculpture which Don Giovanni invited to dinner is described in Malcolm Baker's 'Odzooks! A Man of Stone' (p. 62).

The same spirit of scientific rationalism which led to the cataloguing of lives and deaths was used in the eighteenth century to justify permissiveness itself – at least in England – as Roy Porter describes in 'Libertinism and Promiscuity' (p. 1). 'Bodily functions' came to be seen as 'designed for human benefit'; 'sex could now be regarded as socially positive', indeed a prerequisite of health. And this not only for the men. ' "The appellation of rake is as genteel in a woman as a man of quality", tartly commented Lady Mary Wortley Montagu, and many ladies thought that what was sauce for the gander ought to be sauce for the goose.'

Nor should we see the role of the women in the opera purely as victim. Their appearances are no less ambiguous than any other aspect of *Don Giovanni*. In 'The Seductions of Women' (p. 48), Jane Miller suggests that the very language in which stories of seduction are told implies the collusion of women: even those stories which are told by, or on behalf of women. Even more disturbing is Laclos's Marquise de Merteuil, who, to wreak her revenge on the treacherous male species, adopts Juanesque strategies herself that denigrate her own sex, as Marina Warner points out:

> Her own male protectors dead, a widow without parents or children, she plays with women too, like Don Juan, in order to humiliate and disempower men; she has taken up occupation of a masculine place in the code of chivalry, and her scheming and pursuits seem in the novel all the more diabolical for this trespass across the boundaries of gender.

Change, in sexual and social custom, in the philosophical representation of the world, in religious conviction, is a driving force of *Don Giovanni*. The Don becomes, in effect, the existential hero who declares – even beyond his intransigent sexuality – that 'no rules which have so far prevailed will bind me'. But is he a hero, or is he merely an unprincipled villain, gratifying his feelings at the expense of others? Joseph Kerman, echoing Wye Jamison Allanbrook, argues that the Don is 'No-Man', that at the heart of the opera is a 'void', and that opera's most irresistible seducer is also the least inventive character musically. To borrow Kierkegaard's phrase, how, then, do we account for *Don Giovanni*'s 'great and unsettling power'?

Equivocation is once again at the very heart of the work. At every turn a rich, indefinable territory. The essays which follow explore some of the paths, historical, mythological, sociological and psychological that lead into the depths.

DON GIOVANNI

Libertinism and Promiscuity

ROY PORTER

'Where is male chastity to be found?' expostulated John Wesley: 'Amongst the nobility, among the gentry, among the tradesmen, or among the common people of England? How few can lay claim to it at all?' For preachers to condemn fornication is, of course, nothing new, and yet something is noteworthy in Wesley's accusation, for he accurately pinpointed the extraordinary ubiquity of sexual licence in his lifetime. Other eras had had their notorious pockets of immorality, their courts of voluptuaries, their wenching warriors, their wandering scholars chanting the *Carmina Burana*, or a peasantry still wedded more to carnival than to Christianity. Yet in the age of Wesley – the age of Mozart – commentators the length and breadth of Europe were struck by the universal profligacy which seemed to be infecting all ranks and sectors of society.[1]

In England, for example, George II was routinely portrayed in political cartoons fondling his mistresses, and a couple of generations later, the sons of George III, the Prince Regent especially, were to set new native standards for royal philandering (though none was in the same league as Augustus the Strong, Elector of Saxony and King of Poland, who sired 354 acknowledged bastards). A rung or two down the social scale, polite society carried on its adulteries, liaisons, and complex ménages with a brazen assurance hitherto unmatched. Even the worldly-wise Horace Walpole was slightly surprised, when he dined with Lancelot Blackburne, Archbishop of York, to find that the prelate's mistress, Mrs Cruys, sat at the head of the table, while at the bottom was Mr Hayter, his son by another mistress, who officiated as chaplain, *en route* to becoming Bishop of London. Similarly, Lady Harley reputedly had children by so many men that her brood came to be known as the 'Harleian Miscellany'. 'No one is shocked', bemoaned Lady Mary Wortley Montagu, 'to hear that Miss So-and-So, Maid of Honour, has got nicely over her confinement.'

Further down, similar values were common. In late eighteenth-century London, Francis Place observed how open were sexual pursuits: brothels, pornographic print shops and prostitutes all abounded. How easy was the virtue of man and woman alike! His landlord's family offered a good example:[2]

> His eldest daughter was and had been for several years a common prostitute. His youngest daughter, who was about seventeen years of age, had genteel lodgings where she was visited by gentlemen; and the second daughter . . . was kept by a captain of an East India ship, in whose absence she used to amuse herself as such women generally do.

And this sort of permissiveness showed itself equally among the lower orders at large. The popular picture of a rumbustious Rabelaisian peasantry frolicking time out of mind in the haystacks is almost certainly erroneous; village communities, overseen by lord and parson and terrified of scarcity, had traditionally enforced strict sexual continence. But the soaring bastardy figures in town and country alike during the eighteenth century tell another tale. For a variety of reasons, men and women were growing less vigilant about avoiding children born out of wedlock.

And if Wesley was right that the chaste male was a rare bird, he was also surely correct – even if he exaggerated – to go on to claim: 'How few desire so much as the reputation of it! How numerous are they now even among such as are accounted men of honour and probity who are as fed horses, every one neighing after his neighbour's wife.' Of course, in choice circles, a name for being a bit of a blade had always gone down well. At Charles II's court, Lord Guildford was advised 'to keep a whore', because 'he was ill looked upon for want of doing so'. But lax sexual morals – sowing wild oats, frequenting street-women, keeping mistresses – found remarkable acceptance in eighteenth-century milieux, even amongst the respectable. In having Squire Western put it to Sophy, apropos of Tom Jones's philandering,

> you have not the worse opinion of a young fellow for getting a bastard, have you, girl? No, no, the women will like un the better for't

Fielding was obviously laying it on a bit thick. Yet Boswell was informed by the Honourable Mrs Stuart that

> from what she had seen of life in this great town she would not be uneasy at an occasional infidelity in her husband, as she did not think it at all connected with affection . . . a transient fancy for a girl, or being led by one's companions after drinking to an improper place, was not to be considerered as inconsistent with true affection.

Dr Johnson thought sensible wives should turn a blind eye to their husbands' adulteries (as no bastards were imposed upon them, no real harm was done), and many wives did just that. When Cecilia Thrale's husband started sleeping with his maid, she shrugged it off: 'It is the way, and all who understand genteel life think lightly of such matters'. And when Boswell himself told his wife Margaret he must 'have a concubine', she replied that he 'might go to whom he pleased', prepared, it seems, to put up with his endless infidelities, so long as he didn't pox her.

Boswell's appetites were indeed extraordinary. During the 1760s he made three married women his mistresses, had liaisons with four actresses, kept three lower class mistresses and recorded having sex with over sixty different prostitutes. Few males can have been so promiscuous.[3] And the double standard certainly ensured that licence and indulgence of this order were not readily granted to respectable women. Thus, when Boswell's Dutch sweetheart, Zélide, told him she would 'like to have a husband who could let her go away sometimes to amuse herself', Boswell was furious: 'she seemed a frantic libertine'. Yet sampling the pleasures of the flesh was not a male-only sport. Pope evoked traditional misogyny when he wrote, 'Ev'ry woman is at heart a rake', yet certain fashionable ladies were quite prepared to live up to, or rather down to, that judgment. 'The appellation of rake is as genteel in a woman as a man of quality', tartly commented Lady Mary Wortley Montagu, and many ladies thought that what was sauce for the gander ought to be sauce for the goose. As one of Boswell's lady friends put it to him, marriage

> is merely a mutual contract which if one party breaks, the other is free. 'Now', said she, 'my husband I know has been unfaithful to me a thousand times. I should therefore have no scruple of conscience, I do declare, to have an intrigue'. . . . I argued the chastity of women was of much more consequence than that of men, as the property and rights of families depend upon it. 'Surely' said she, 'that is easily answered, for the objection is removed if a woman does not intrigue but when she is with child.'[4]

(Lamely, Boswell reflected that he thought 'she was wrong', but he 'really could not answer her'.) Certainly the charmed circle of society mistresses and *demi-mondaines* achieved greater éclat and respect than in any previous era, and modest ladies might have been pardoned for thinking that the way for their sex to get on was through a generous yet judicious bestowal of sexual favours.

Europe was a Christian civilization; the Church was fundamentally suspicious of the pleasures of the flesh, lust was a deadly sin, and the Commandments forbade adultery. Moralists likewise denounced debauchery: in his print sequence, Hogarth showed how the Rake's Progress led inexorably to the madhouse and the Harlot's Progress to death. Moreover, it was a society (historians have recently argued) in which upper class matrimony was ceasing to be a matter of dynastic convenience, and was becoming more a match of sentiment and love. Yet in this environment, promiscuity seemed more flagrant, more tolerated than ever before.

Why was this? Doubtless the cajoling of Reformation religious fanaticism was important; doubtless the relative stability of late *ancien régime* society allowed some relaxation of moral vigilance. The pursuit of ease, elegance, and fashion amongst a leisured élite encouraged experimentation with exciting new life styles, while, among common folk, the prospect of more mouths to feed thanks to sexual gallivanting was made less daunting by economic expansion.

But how, in that Christian civilization, within which family stability was the foundation of the social order, did those who engaged in promiscuity – sexual behaviour which threatened that very order which made licence possible – justify their actions?

Many, of course, then – as before, as now – never did. Who knows how many men and women took liberties, knowing full well they were acting viciously or sinfully, and just got away with it, or got caught, as chance would have it? Yet there was also a different strand in the Age of the Enlightenment. For in matters sexual no less than in questions of politics or religion, many were now criticizing received authority and the old ways, and struggling to reason out new experiments in living. In an atmosphere of philosophical and tea-table debate, reflected and dramatized on the stage and in fiction, articulate people puzzled out their views on sin, sex, and sensibility, at all levels from triumphant ratiocination to *post coitum* excuses.

Libertinism was nothing new, and traditions of free thought defying and parodying orthodox Christianity had long lineages. In the sixteenth century, Rabelais had turned Christian teachings upside down in a gross, grotesque anarchic carnival, while Renaissance poets drew on Ovid and urged: *carpe diem*, or gather ye rose buds while ye may:

> Come my Celia, let us prove
> While we can the sports of love.

And then, particularly in the seventeenth century, an aggressive philosophical libertinism was uttered by *esprits forts* who despised Catholicism as a warped clerical conspiracy, turning to obscenity to express their sense of the obscenity of the Church's own prohibitions. In seventeenth-century France and Restoration England bold spirits combined blasphemy and pornography in such exposés as *l'Ecole des Filles*, *Venus in the Cloister*, and *La Religieuse* (Diderot's exposé of the sex life of the convent), a genre which flourished throughout the Enlightenment.

In real life, eighteenth-century libertinism took many forms. It could appear as the shameless chauvinistic manipulation of power and privilege for selfish gratification exemplified by the notorious early Georgian rake, Francis Charteris, whose career actually culminated in a rape conviction (he received a royal pardon). His obituary described him as a man

> Who with an inflexible Constancy,
> And inimitable uniformity of Life,
> Persisted, in spight of Age and Infirmity,
> In the Practice of every Human Vice,
> Excepting Prodigality and Hypocrisy;
> His insatiable Avarice
> Exempting him from the first,
> And his matchless Impudence
> From the latter.

Or it could take the ultimate form of the desperate nihilism of de Sade, acting out his own defiance of an evil cosmos through the exhaustive victimization of the body. Or it could express itself through the cavortings of gentlemanly English rakehells such as John Wilkes, Lord Sandwich and Sir Francis Dashwood, amusing themselves dressed up as monks engaging in orgiastic blasphemous rites at Medmenham Abbey, a sort of dummy run for Genet's *Balcony*.

While some of these may be dismissed merely as isolated monsters, they operated never the less in the context of a widespread ferment of opinion among those for whom the *ex cathedra* morality of the Church and traditional institutions now offered false frameworks for sexual values, or at least ones which squared ill with their own instincts. By exploring this 'popular', as distinct from 'heroic', libertinism we may actually tune in to Don Giovanni and his desires.

What made this diluted libertinism palatable to ordinary eighteenth-century minds, made it seem sense not sin, was, of course, that fundamental liberalization of Christianity codified by seventeenth-century rationalism and the Scientific Revolution. The old Augustinian theology, built upon Original Sin, had intimately linked the world, the flesh and the devil, and attributed man's fallen state to the carnal knowledge of Adam and Eve. But this way of thinking had now lost its near-universal hold on people's minds. Christians newly proclaimed the goodness of Nature under a benevolent Deity. Bodily functions and natural desires (as personally experienced and also as theorized by medicine) must therefore, philosophers argued, not be marks of sin but rather designed for human benefit. Hence sex, far from being a snare or just a clumsy mechanism of generation (Sir Thomas Browne had wished humans could propagate like trees) could become desirable in itself and praised as a source of gratification. As the Scotsman Robert Wallace put it, 'The Venereal Act . . . when it is performed in obedience to nature' is 'highly delightful'. Indeed, sex could now be regarded as socially positive rather than disruptive: erotic attraction, thought David Hume, was the 'first and original principle of human society', as also of aesthetics. Indeed, it was the very quintessence of happiness. 'Animal attraction', judged Dr Erasmus Darwin, Charles's grandfather, was 'the purest source of human felicity, the cordial drop in the otherwise vapid cup of life'.[5]

This revaluation of sexuality was reinforced by the advance of physiology. Anatomists researching the nervous system came to see the senses and the genitals, the brain and the mind as forming a single integrated system. The age-old Platonic and Augustinian doctrines of the civil war of Mind against the passions – including sex – yielded to new visions of an intimate dialectic integrating sensation, sex, sensibility and consciousness. In France, Condillac derived thinking from touching and, pursuing a parallel tack, Erasmus Darwin argued that the sense of beauty took its origin from infants' experience of the 'female bosom'.

Not least, medical science contended that an active sex life was necessary to enjoy the bloom of health. Erasmus Darwin and many other physicians prescribed love-making as a remedy for psychosomatic disorders such as hypochondria, and the pioneer sex therapist James Graham believed that sexual lethargy was both symptom and cause of the sickness of advanced nations at large. Sex and health became intimately associated. When Samuel Johnson caught his old medical friend, Dr Robert James, with a whore, James explained 'that he always took a swelling in his stones [i.e. testicles] if he abstained a month'. Similarly Lord Carlisle noted: 'I was afraid I was going to have an attack of gout the other day; I believe I live too chaste. 'Tis not a common fault with me.' Overall Enlightenment ideas often came close to identifying sexual desire with the life force itself. Within Erasmus Darwin's pioneering evolutionary theory, Eros was the '*chef d'œuvre*, the master piece of nature', which animated biological progress.

Mainline eighteenth-century thought thus came to regard sex as thoroughly natural, indeed as forming the soul of nature itself. It was a universal desire or hunger (in *Tom Jones* Fielding wrote of 'the Desire of satisfying a voracious Appetite with a certain Quantity of delicate white human Flesh'). And it was the supreme source of pleasure ('in my mind', reflected Boswell, 'there cannot be higher felicity on earth enjoyed by man than the participation of genuine reciprocal amorous affection with an amiable woman'). Moreover, this new sense of the rightness, the *right* of free sexual expression, as doing what comes naturally, was reinforced by a range of contemporary experiences and outlooks.

For example, navigators who explored the Pacific paradise of Tahiti found the natives both extremely generous in spontaneously bestowing sexual favours, yet also happy and socially stable. As later with Margaret Mead's Samoans, Polynesian society was to prove less 'innocent' but, for many Europeans, the Tahitians served as a kind of 'thought experiment', showing how a society could combine erotic freedom ('innocent pleasure') and social harmony, without taboos. Other newly explored 'primitive' societies confirmed the new view that sex could be a social boon not a bane. Among Eskimos, for instance, it was discovered that shamans healed and performed rites of passage through sexual initiation. And such revelations soon found their sensational echoes back home. The London madam, Mrs Hayes, ran shows advertised as the celebration of Tahitian rites:

> this evening at 7 o'clock precisely 12 beautiful nymphs, spotless virgins, will carry out the famous Feast of Venus as it is celebrated in Tahiti, under the instruction and leadership of Queen Oberea (which role will be taken by Mrs Hayes herself).

The idea that Tahiti represented humanity's 'natural' state had notable implications. The Enlightenment's attempts to deduce the rise of civilized society from a primitive state of nature seemed to require an initial stage in which natives had casually copulated just as they instinctually satisfied their need for food or drink. The moral of such 'just so' stories (as later with Freud's myth of the primitive horde in *Totem and Taboo*) was that the transition from 'rudeness' to 'refinement', from copulation through polygamy to monogamy, was a matter largely of social convention. Tracing the roots of sexual institutions and taboos easily served to undermine them. Vico, for example, located the origins of marriage by suggesting that the primeval 'giants', dreading the wrath of the gods, had grown ashamed of casual copulation in public, and had taken instead to dragging off one particular woman into the privacy of a cave, and keeping her there: 'In this guise marriage was introduced, which is a chaste carnal union consummated under the fear of some divinity'. If monogamy was so grotesque in its origins, why not slough off such benighted institutions and return to nature?

All in all, the Enlightenment exploration of nature – through science, geography and history – helped create visions of marriage and monogamy as conventional at best, at worst arbitrarily serving false ends (e.g. property transfer) rather than human joy. So although Bernard Mandeville, in both his *Fable of the Bees* and his *Defence of the Public Stews*, supported matrimony as a desirable social convention, yet – here was the sting in its tail – he believed that given human nature, marriage would mop up only a portion of male desires: 'As long as it is the Nature of Man . . . to have a Salt Itch under the breeches, the Brimstone under the Petticoat will be necessary to lay it.' Hence public brothels would be necessary as a further institution to ensure that surplus lust didn't debauch the respectable. Contemporaneously, Defoe's Moll Flanders treated chastity as a mere artifice: 'whether he intended to Marry me, or not to Marry me, seem'd a Matter of no great Consequence to me'.

In such a climate, desire assumed a primacy; pursuing desire, though deemed a vice or sin, seemed to many the natural course of action unless countered by some weightier obstacle. 'The order of Nature is to follow my appetite,' wrote the Restoration playwright, John Crowne, 'am I to eat at Noon because it is noon or because I am hungry?', or as Boswell phrased it, 'I considered indulgence with women to be like any other indulgence of nature.' Thus desire viewed as *primum mobile* blazed a trail for promiscuity. On the one hand, it encouraged people to think of the libido as sovereign, beyond human control because part of the mechanical order of nature, governed only by cosmic laws of matter and motion. In John Cleland's novel *Memoirs of a Woman of Pleasure* ('*Fanny Hill*'), desire itself seems to be a physical force, with sexual arousal and sexual release often represented by the metaphors of hydraulics.[6] It could also be seen as a raging passion provoked by female beauty or the mere sight of the genitals. Thus many protests were raised against the new profession of male obstetrician on the grounds that the intimate contact involved between the doctor and female genitalia must inevitably provoke sexual eruption: 'If men midwives under these circumstances stand unmoved, they are a part of the human species I am a stranger to!'

Then again, Nature, as science showed, was all motion. Did not that argue for human sexual mobility too – the pursuit of gratification wherever it could be found? If desires were fluid, why should not gratification be diversified and multiplied? Don Giovanni's list, which had reached 2065, was marked by its restless diversity:

Among these there are countrywomen, chambermaids, city-women, there are countesses, baronesses, marchionesses, princesses, and there are women of every rank, of every shape, of every age!

But long before, Molière's Dom Juan, able to 'refuse nothing to a pretty face', had explained how crucial were novelty and change: 'the excitement of fresh desire – I can't explain it, but for me all the pleasures of love is in variety' (though, unlike Mozart's, Molière's Dom Juan confessed to the tedium of sameness). And Macheath, hero of *The Beggar's Opera*, used a similar erotic arithmetic for counting the sum of human happiness: 'I love the sex; and a man who loves money might as well be contented with one guinea, as I with one woman'.

Thus the pursuit of pleasure became the fulfilment of Nature, unfettered by arbitrary bugbears. And if happiness resulted, what wrong could there be? Hence, within this apologia for libertinism, the criterion of harm was all important. Fielding had his Tom Jones vindicate his wild oats in this way: 'I have been guilty with women, I own it; but am not conscious that I have ever injured any – nor would I, to procure pleasure to myself, be knowingly the cause of misery to any human being'. And such disclaimers – excuses, it is true, but excuses with the ring of sincerity – were common enough in real life. Early in the eighteenth century the young man-about-town, Dudley Ryder, justified himself on the grounds that 'a connection with woman . . . when indulged without invading any man's right or any woman's virtue [is] a venial offence arising from a most natural desire'. And Boswell too thought likewise, boasting of his own principle 'of never debauching an innocent girl', though he remained somewhat uneasy about his affairs with married women. Here, however, his mind was put somewhat at rest because he found how eager the women themselves were for such encounters, as Pepys had found a century earlier. A propos of the lusty Mrs Bagwell, Pepys had remarked – hypocrite as ever! – 'strange it is to see how a woman, notwithstanding her great pretence of love to her husband and religion, may be conquered', though clearly this last word needs inverted commas for reasons that anticipated the 'conquest' of Molly Segrim by Tom Jones (Molly, Fielding writes, 'so well played her Part, that Jones attributed the Conquest entirely to himself'). Contemporary fiction was also full of lecherous women such as Widow Wadman in *Tristram Shandy*, and the diaries of men such as Boswell, the Scottish footman John MacDonald, and William Hickey make it clear that they did not find it difficult to get respectable women, and not just whores, to go to bed with them.

Thus a libertinism, based on instinct, freedom, and the pursuit of pleasure under the aegis of a benevolent Nature, became a common ideological currency during the eighteenth century. But the culture of libertinism was richer than that, and its apologia for erotic emancipation drew heavily upon a range of eligible roles which the seducer could adopt. Easily the most common part was that of conqueror. In real life and in fiction, amorous encounters were cast time and again in the metaphors of a war of the sexes, in which it was the male role to contest, lay siege, overcome and gain a victory. In particular, within a sexual etiquette in which virtuous ladies were meant, out of modesty, to resist sexual overtures, men had at least to be psychologically forceful in order to carry their campaigns to successful conclusions. When the force became physical, the seduction turned into rape.[7]

Undoubtedly, the libertine as erotic hero was often odious. The whole notion of conquest highlighted gross sexual inequalities, as well as reflecting wider values – in politics, statecraft, imperial and commercial expansion – which esteemed men in proportion to their aggression. Winning control over women, indeed, crushing and humiliating them, was the main goal in some libertine strategies (Lovelace in *Clarissa Harlowe* comes to mind), leading Taine to reflect in the nineteenth century how, in contrast to the instinctive sensuality of the Mediterranean rake, his English equivalent was cold and proud, driven by a lust to dominate.[8]

Yet a word of qualification is necessary. From *The Rape of the Lock* and Sterne's Corporal Trim to Boswell's fantasies of being Captain Plume or Macheath, much 'conquest' talk was essentially playful in tone. In any case, as Tom Jones's 'conquest' of Molly

Segrim suggests, women themselves could stage-manage 'conquests', or simply treat the would-be erotic Alexander as a joke (quite the most ludicrous man in the whole of Jane Austen is Sir Edward in *Sanditon* whose 'great object in life was to be seductive').

Linked to the role of conqueror was that of Turk. Islam above all presented an advanced society in which polygamy was lawful. Not surprisingly then, the Turk with his seraglio preoccupied the libertine imagination. Both the notorious rake, Lord Baltimore, and Edward Wortley Montagu (who actually converted to Islam) reputedly kept their own harems, and William Douglas ('Old Q'), the rake of Piccadilly, was said to live in 'oriental voluptuousness'. In lambasting male midwives, the worst charge that Philip Thicknesse could lay at their door was that they raised the spectre of Islamic sexuality ('I never met any of these obstetrical physicians, that I do not look on them, as I should on the Emperor of Morocco or the Bashaw of Tangier, going to his seraglio'). Yet, for many, the image had real attraction: 'I am too changeable where women are concerned', confessed Boswell, allured by 'Asiatic ideas', 'I ought to be a Turk'. Once again, however, a certain element of self-parody intrudes. The point at which Captain Macheath compared himself to a Turk:

> Thus I stand like a Turk, with his doxies around,
> From all sides their glances his passion confound;
> For black, brown, and fair, his inconstancy burns,
> And the different beauties subdue him by turns;

was the moment when he was about to be hanged.

Other roles occasionally commended themselves to those trying to justify their promiscuous urges. Men sometimes fancied themselves as Jove or Bacchus, and Richardson's Lovelace compared himself to Aeneas and Tarquin. But the most powerful authorization was none other than Christianity itself. Fringe sects in the seventeenth century had argued that to the pure all things are pure, and on that basis had called for free love for free spirits (Abiezer Coppe, the Ranter leader, urged, 'Give over thy stinking family duties'). And eighteenth-century blasphemous pornography linked to celebrate God's sexual bounty to mankind, as in the parody hymn:[9]

> What Seed my God's free Bounty gives,
> Let me not frig away;
> For God is paid when Cunt receives,
> T'enjoy is to obey.
> Yet not one Cunt's contracted Span
> My Vigour e'er shall bound;
> I'll think they all were made for Man,
> When thousand Cunts are round.

But the serious argument was Biblical. Old Testament patricians had been polygamous: did not then Scripture sanction the institution? Boswell himself told Rousseau, 'I should like to follow the example of the old Patriarchs, worthy men whose memory I hold in respect' (one side-benefit, Boswell explained, was that 'propagation is thus increased'). It was a possibility to which he returned again and again. He explained to his friend Temple that:

> no man was ever more attached to his wife than I was, but that I had an exuberance of amorous faculties, quite corporeal and unconnected with affection and regard, and that my wife was moderate and averse to too much dalliance. Why might I not then be patriarchal?

He even took up the issue with his wife. He argued that he had Biblical sanction for his needs for a concubine:[10]

> . . . but I was not clear, for though our Saviour did not prohibit concubinage, yet the strain of the New Testament seems to be against it, and the Church had understood it so. My passion, or appetite rather, was so strong that I was inclined to a laxity of interpretation, and . . . thought that I might be like a patriarch;

or rather, I thought that I might enjoy some of my former female acquaintances in London.

Boswell was by no means alone in his 'patriarchal attitudes'. A Scottish minister, the Reverend Daniel Maclauchlan, published in 1735 a similar call for sexual patriarchalism in his *An Essay upon Improving and Adding to the Strength of Great-Britain and Ireland, by Fornication, justifying The same from Scripture and Reason. By a Young Clergyman*. It should, argued Maclauchlan, 'be the great Business of our Lives to Plant and Propagate our Kind. To throw our Seed into every fruitful Corner. To get it vigorously into the gaping Bottom of every sweet-watered Vale . . .'. But most notoriously, in 1780, the chaplain to the London VD Hospital, the Reverend Martin Madan, brought out his *Thelyphthora*, which like-wise argued for the restoration of patriarchal polygamy. It would, he thought, kill several birds with one stone, ending male frustration, giving all women the chance to marry, and putting a stop to prostitution and de-bauchery.

For some, this sense of a divine calling to reseed the nation went beyond theory into practice. A fascinating glimpse is afforded by the diary of Goodwin Wharton, younger brother of the late seventeenth-century Whig Junto leader, Tom Wharton, and important politician in his own right, yet (as his manuscript autobiography shows) a man of quite peculiar inner conscious-ness. Under the influence of his mistress and medium, Mary Parish, Wharton came to believe that God had marked him out as the new Messiah. In the light of that, Wharton found his unsatisfactory sex life with her rather perplexing. For Mary didn't come to lie with him every night, and he found that a few days' enforced abstinence resulted in the discomfort of 'an unimaginable quantity of seed'. To solve these problems, he tried brief encounters – he bedded Mary's friend, Mrs Wilder (or rather, he noted in his diary, she bedded him, since she leapt upon him even before he'd finished propositioning her) and then on a trip to Bath his landlady too (and she too, like the original Wife of Bath, was beside herself with desire for him). But both episodes left him poxed, and led to anguished scenes with the outraged Mary.

Racked by sexual torments, Wharton prayed for heavenly guidance. The divine answer came back loud and clear with instructions even conveniently numerically tabulated:

1 Swear not at all
2 Fuck (every weeke) where you used to do (here Wharton interjects, 'at this broad word (as we call it) my thought stuck, as if I had not rightly understood it; upon which, it was repeated and then was added')
3 That is, give to her her due and then, as Wharton puts it, 'thinking suddenly on the unruly rise of the flesh,' it was added:
4 Throw water on yourself, so shall the Lord prosper you.

Pondering the heavenly precepts, or rather the divine vernacular, Wharton explained that, on reflection, God's use of the broad expression seemed proper: 'the God of nature, I hope, may be allowed to speake plainly of all things whatever . . . I hope I need not plead for God further; who dare accuse or censure Him?'

Wharton's problem remained to decide where exactly his service was due. Clearly with his mistress, Mary, but also, surely, with those other great ladies of the realm whom the spiritual voices he heard in his dreams told him he should lie with as befitted the King of Kings. First, there was James II's spouse, Mary of Modena, who providentially, was childless. Obviously God intended Wharton to give her an heir, at which point, he presumed, James II would abdicate out of gratitude, Wharton would replace him, and he would reconvert the court from Papacy to Protestantism. When Mary ignored his advances, he took it, Malvolio-like, as a come-on, a sign of just how smitten she was.

James speedily fell (God's punishment for his neglect of Wharton's deserts), to be succeeded by William of Orange. Wharton soon discovered that the Dutchman's wife, Queen Mary, was also providentially infatuated with him; he paid her court, and when she fell desperately ill with smallpox, he seized his chance. Commandeering spiritual aid, he would cure her, and melting with gratitude she would admit him to her bed. Unaccountably, however, she died. But when William himself perished soon after (a further divine blow, to smite him for his failure to advance Wharton), Goodwin knew his day at last had come, for while yet a princess, Anne, now Queen Anne, had long been eyeing him up. Once more, death intervened, though this time it was Wharton's.

It is not easy to assess the history of libertinism, for it is difficult to sift myth from reality, literary stereotype and fiction from real life. We can read bawdy ballads and novels, satires and philosophical arguments, but when it comes to grasping what real-life adventurers thought and did, the evidence is all too patchy, and is utterly male-dominated. Certainly one key dimension of libertinism was that cast of mind, starting with the blasphemies of antireligious *esprits forts* of seventeeth-century France and culminating in the 'love of ruins' of Laclos and above all de Sade, whose goal was less sexual pleasure than the liberation which would come from the exposure of hypocrisy, the destruction of illusions, and, ultimately, the naked pursuit of evil. But in the wider annals of libertinism that mode of Satanic nihilism was a minority tradition, which little helps to explain the wider cultivation of erotic hedonism. As a key to that, Casanova's maxim surely carries greater weight: 'To cultivate the pleasures of my senses was throughout my life my main preoccupation; I have never had any more important objective.' That is a view embodied, in its inevitably messy way, in the raking career of men like Boswell, and best expressed in Georgian England in the sentiments of *Fanny Hill*, with its comprehensive vision of erotic pleasure as a good to be sought, acquired, traded and maximized, and its denial of the ultimate reality of evil or pain. In the libertine fantasy of *Fanny Hill* you can have your cake and eat it, indeed, in as many different ways as you please. And there is a happy ending. The gratification of Eros proves wholly compatible with romantic love ('Reader, I married him', applied to Fanny long before Jane Eyre). The Harlot's Progress was ever upwards.

We might not expect this bourgeois pleasure principle to relate to Don Giovanni, yet is he so very different from Fanny Hill, in his capacity to pursue and to bestow erotic pleasure?[11] As Kierkegaard recognized, what animated the Don was not the urge to ruin and avenge but a 'power of desire, the energy of sensual desire'. Certainly, in their different ways, both Stendhal and Goethe were to find Don Giovanni's endless urge to repeat, his failure to go beyond the pleasure principle, merely boring, dismal and sterile, rather as today's Freudians might find it infantile and neurotic. Romanticism needs the Don to be disappointed, and so to change, seek redemption, and maybe find grace; in short, to be Faust. Yet these Romantic and psychoanalytic critiques of hedonism do not necessarily illuminate the world of the Don. Nor did these more modern myths necessarily constitute a higher wisdom. On the brink of the twenty-first century, in an age when an unprecedented hedonism had been, for many, the only god, we do not find the eighteenth-century libertine so remote, nor his philosophies unthinkable.

Notes to Libertinism and Promiscuity

1 I shall not give full references in this piece for matters of fact and brief quotations. I am much indebted to several recent works in this area for discussion and information, in particular Lawrence Stone, *The family, sex and marriage in England 1500 – 1800* (London, 1976); P.-G. Boucé (ed.), *Sexuality in eighteenth century Britain* (Manchester, 1982); I. Bloch, *A history of English sexual morals* (London, 1958); Roger Thompson, *Unfit for modest ears* (London, 1979); G.S. Rousseau and Roy Porter (eds.), *Sexual underworlds of the Enlightenment* (Manchester, 1987). I hope to publish a fuller account of eighteenth-century sexuality in its medical context in the near future.

2 Mary Thale (ed.), *The autobiography of Francis Place* (Cambridge, 1972), p. 71.

3 Particularly good on Boswell's sex life is Stone's discussion in *Family, sex and marriage*, pp. 580f.

4 Quoted in Stone, *Family, sex and marriage*, p. 506.

5 See Roy Porter, 'Mixed feelings: the Enlightenment and sexuality in eighteenth century Britain', in P.-G. Boucé (ed.), *Sexuality*, pp. 1–27.

6 There are good discussions of Cleland's mechanical ideas of sex in the introduction to two recent editions of the *Memoirs*, one by Peter Sabor in the World's Classics series, and the other by Peter Wagner in the Penguin edition.

7 See John Forrester, 'Rape, Seduction and Psychoanalysis', and Roy Porter, 'Rape – Does it have a historical meaning?', both in Sylvana Tomaselli and Roy Porter (eds.), *Rape* (Oxford, 1986); and R. Folkenflik (ed.), *The English hero, 1660–1800* (Newark, London & Toronto, 1982).

8 Quoted in Bloch, *English sexual morals*, p. 276.

9 See A. Hamilton, *The Infamous Essay on Women* (London, 1972), p. 237.

10 C. Ryskamp and F. A. Pottle (eds.), *Boswell. The ominous years, 1774–1776* (New York, 1963), p. 74.

11 W. H. Epstein, *John Cleland. Images of a Life* (New York, 1974).

Don Juanism from Below

ROBERT DARNTON

Don Juans belong to the upper classes. A Leporello may leer at a peasant girl or paw at a lady if properly disguised, but he cannot practise the noble art of seduction, at least not on the stage. But what happened off stage? Was there a plebeian variety of Don Juanism? No scholar, however partial to the Pompadour style of socio-cultural history, would deny a sex life to the working man. Workers also had sexual fantasies, as witness Restif de la Bretonne. If we take Don Juanism as a compound of sex (one part) and fantasy (nine parts), we might expect it to have flourished among the working classes in the age of Mozart. But we know very little about it. In fact our knowledge hardly extends beyond one document, *Journal de ma vie*, the autobiography of a Parisian glazier named Jacques Ménétra.[1]

But what a document! Ménétra's autobiography reads like a historian's dream come true. It fits perfectly into the current picture of Old Regime demography (Ménétra married at twenty-seven and had four children of whom two died in infancy). It also conforms to the standard view of the sans-culotte (Ménétra worked with his hands but earned enough as an independent artisan to support a family.) And best of all, it is told in Ménétra's own words. It conveys his understanding of what it meant to grow up among the *menu peuple* in Paris, where he was born in 1738; to tramp around provincial shops on a journeyman's *tour de France*; to settle down with a shop and family of his own; and to live through the great events of the Revolution as a militant in a Parisian Section.

It seems astonishing that such a manuscript should turn up after being buried for nearly two centuries. But four other working-class autobiographies from the Old Regime have surfaced in the last few years,[2] and others may still be lying undiscovered in attics and archives. The autobiographical urge extended far deeper in French society than we had suspected.

So did skirt-chasing. The two urges were connected in Ménétra's case, for he presents his life as a chase after skirts. Although he picked up some knowledge of his craft on his *tour de France*, he mainly picked up girls, or so he would have us believe. He narrates his travels as a series of seductions strung out in geographical order: the juicy *bourgeoise* in Vendôme; the lusty farmer's wife in Luynes; the saddler's wife in Tours; the servant girl in Angers; the plump widow in Nantes; the whore upended in the moat of Bordeaux; the lascivious nuns of Agen; the merry widows of Toulouse and Nîmes; the pregnant button-maker in Carpentras; the overripe matron in Lyons; the mother–daughter combination in Bourg-en-Bresse; the waitress in Auxerre, 'big and naughty and with a good appetite'. And so on and so on. Ménétra's list does not stretch as far as Leporello's, but it is impressive: fifty-two seductions before his wedding and a dozen afterwards, not counting liaisons with prostitutes.

Like Leporello's master, Ménétra hunted 'female game', as he put it, of all variety – 'the pretty laundress' and the love-starved noblewoman 'in her charms just about the way Venus looks in paintings'; the innocent country girl 'as beautiful as love' and the Parisian whore 'with a great deal of temperament'. Ménétra confessed to a special inclination for nuns: 'Ah what pleasure for a mortal to devour the flesh of the Lord in his harem'. And he liked his flesh fat: 'She was charming, fat, well larded'.

Ménétra loved the hunt itself, the chase more than the skirt. Having cornered his quarry – in the hayloft, behind the barrel, or between the sheets – words seem to fail him, at least in his narrative. Not that he feels constrained by literary niceties. He rejects the conventions of high literature, including even punctuation, so that his conquests flow by in an uninterrupted *roman-fleuve* of 250 pages. But when the critical moment comes, he finds nothing to say or falls back on clichés: 'ecstasy', 'sweet inebriation'; 'I thought I was where the gods are in one of those moments when we believe we have become their equal'. Once in bed, all women are equal, except for some differences in 'temperament'. They cease to be interesting. It is seduction, not fornication, that counts.

Being endlessly varied, seduction provides limitless matter for stories, and stories are essential to Don Juanism. If the Dons lack a Leporello, they will recount their conquests by themselves. For their 'ism' is less a pattern of behaviour than a kind of narrative: male braggadocio dressed up as opera and drama, or dressed down as locker-room farce and dirty joking. In Ménétra's case it took the form of autobiography. But what did autobiography mean for a man of the people in eighteenth-century France?

Ménétra did not follow any obvious model. In fact, he broke with literary convention by refusing to divide his story into chapters, paragraphs, or even sentences. Instead of addressing an explicit audience, he dedicated his text to himself ('à mon esprit') and filled it with allusions and expressions that make no sense to the modern reader. But they probably would have produced some belly laughs among his fellow sans-culottes. For Ménétra wrote in a popular idiom, and writing was a part of popular culture in eighteenth-century Paris.

Paris had about 500 free elementary schools – one for every 1200 inhabitants – in Ménétra's day. He mentions as a matter of course that he learned the three r's and singing in parish schools and that he and his companions on the *tour de France* frequently wrote letters to keep in touch with their families, to court their women, and to find out about jobs farther down the road. When Ménétra tramped, he carried a book in the sack slung over his back. When he settled in a town, he improvised songs and staged skits with other workers. Back in Paris, he spent many evenings in the boulevard theatres. He often went drinking with vaudeville stars like Gaspard Taconnet, an actor and author of *poissard* farces, and Pierre Gourlin, a popular harlequin. Literature and the written word belonged to his daily life, so it does not seem incredible that he should put his life into writing. Ménétra needed to make sense of his experience just as much as Rousseau did.

The comparison with Rousseau is difficult to avoid, although Jean-Jacques wrote his way up to the top of society while Ménétra remained unpublished and obscure, a layer or two from the bottom. They actually crossed paths, if Ménétra can be believed. According to his *Journal*, they took walks around Paris together in 1770 and once stopped by the Café de la Régence to play checkers (Rousseau won). Both of them came from humble homes: Rousseau's father was a watchmaker, Ménétra's a glazier. Both lost their mothers as infants. Both had troubled relations with their fathers and spent much of their youth on the road. Both confessed.

But where Rousseau wallowed in guilt, Ménétra boasted. Like Jean-Jacques, he had left a string of illegitimate children behind him, but he was proud of it. He, too, had a weakness for a 'maman', but his ran a whore-house. He was also surrounded by conspirators, but he beat them off with a broom handle. Ménétra swaggered through life with such zest that his *Journal* reads like Rousseau turned upside down and rewritten in the language of the working man: the confessions of a *titi parisien*.

It also can be read as a tall tale. At the outset, Ménétra announces, 'I am going to write about all my pranks.' The theme of joking – *fredaines*, *niches*, *espiègleries* – runs throughout the narrative and provides Ménétra with a way of organizing it. He presents his life as a series of pranks, which all demonstrate the same happy conclusion: no matter what he does, he always comes out on top. He outwits the *mamans* and wins free bed and breakfast in the best brothels of Paris. He seduces the wives of his friends and thus restores domestic tranquillity to some frustrated households. He bamboozles the intendant of Bordeaux and thereby saves his companions from being drafted into the army.

Ménétra triumphs over everything. Small in stature but a 'Hercules in love', he seduces all the girls, wins all the fights, rescues drowning children, puts out fires, dupes yokels, confounds priests, and even buys a surprising share of successful lottery tickets, using the proceeds to regale his friends in the finest taverns and houses of pleasure in Paris. Ménétra is so successful, in fact, that he seems too good to be true.

Much of the *Journal* is patently false. Ménétra could not have exchanged greetings with the folk-hero-bandit Louis Mandrin in 1762, as he claimed, because Mandrin had been executed in 1755. It seems equally unlikely that Ménétra led 500 members of his workers' association, the *compagnonnage du Devoir*, against 750 of the rival *Gavots* in a pitched battle near Angers, leaving seven dead and fifty-seven wounded. Journeymen on the *tour de France* certainly brawled among themselves, but not on such a scale and probably not without leaving a trace of their disturbances in the archives.

Ménétra tells a story about an innkeeper and his wife who inadvertently murdered their son as if it had happened under his nose, but it came from a common *canard* or broadside that peddlers had been hawking in various editions since 1618. He also seems to have plagiarized some of his material about the sex life of the clergy from under-the-cloak classics like *Vénus dans le cloître*, *Dom B. . . . .*, *Portier des Chartreux*, and *La foutromanie*. The popular literature of his time featured many of the things that he passes off as everyday occurrences in his travels: hideous crimes, encounters with ghosts, black magic, dramatic rescues, practical jokes (the funniest at the expense of priests), and orgies (the juiciest in nunneries).

Did Ménétra fabricate his entire *Journal*, or did some hoaxer make up Ménétra? It would be abusive to push one's scepticism too far. Scraps of evidence in the Parisian archives establish the dates of Ménétra's birth (13 July 1738) and marriage (28 June 1765), though not his death (some time after 1802, when his name appears in the *état-civil* for his daughter's marriage). A few references in his account of his *tour de France* – the Battle of Saint-Cast (11 September 1758), the earthquake in Guyenne (10 August 1759) – can be confirmed by outside sources.[3] The whole autobiography gives off an air of authenticity. And where its facts seem unreliable, it is convincing as fantasy. If Ménétra was a Walter Mitty, he shows what eighteenth-century dreams were made of.

But above all he was a story-teller. He even seduced by spinning yarns, an Old Regime variety of what the French refer to today as *baratin* or sweet talk. 'She liked it when I told her stories.' 'I chatted her up and talked of love.' 'I told jokes to the girls and stories to the women.' The *Journal* is composed of tales and of tales within tales. By weaving them together, Ménétra produced a picture of his life. He fabricated the meta-tale of Ménétra the seducer and thus seduces us, his readers.

Lest that sound too fancy, I should point out that story-telling appears as an everyday event in the *Journal*. Workers constantly swapped tales while carousing in taverns, tramping to new jobs, and stopping in inns favoured by their *compagnonnage*. They usually slept two to a bed with several beds in the same room and recounted their adventures before dozing off. The setting – part locker room, part dormitory, all of it suffused with young male swagger – provided an ideal occasion for Ménétra's favourite genre, the sexual yarn. What better way to impress the guys in Toulouse, either before or after blowing out the candle, than to tell them the one about the convent of Agen? The nuns had hired Ménétra to repair their windows, and at first they made him wear a bell so they would be warned of his approach. But once he got under their skirts they took to knitting him stockings. Who in Lyons could top his goodnight story about whoring outside the city walls of Bordeaux? Ménétra had turned his whore over to his one-eyed mate from La Rochelle but neglected to warn him about the flying patrol. So the constabulary snuck up on the Rochelais's blind side and caught him *en flagrant délit*. Sometimes the workers exchanged burlesque 'confessions' about the sins they had committed on the road. Sometimes, like Ulysses, they spun yarns before well-born hosts. After working in a château, Ménétra and a companion were invited to the seigneur's table: 'He took pleasure in getting us to recount all our pranks and everything we had done on our *tour de France*. I told a few stories for them. The seigneur and his wife laughed until the tears ran down their cheeks.'

The *Journal* seems to be an extension of these bull sessions, translated awkwardly into writing in 1764, when Ménétra returned from his last tour of the provinces and drafted the bulk of his manuscript. In sections written later, he provided information about his life after 1765, when he set up his own shop in Paris. But he devoted most of the text to the period that he considered his happiest, the seven years that he spent on the road, with occasional forays back on the boulevards at home.

The modern reader may laugh along with Ménétra's tales from his *tour de France*, because they seem vaguely familiar. We can place them in a narrative tradition that extends from Boccaccio to current jokes about travelling salesmen. Thus the story of the old prude in Lyons, who though deaf was 'still fresh': Ménétra blows out the candle and takes her 'by assault' just before a knock announces her husband. As he enters, Ménétra hides behind the door, 'happy invention'. The wife sends the husband to fetch a new candle. Then Ménétra scrambles into his breeches and down the stairs, dodging the old man on the way. If we did not read it in the *Decameron*, we probably heard a related version around a campfire or at some other gathering of male animals.

But what are we to make of Ménétra's conquest of the peasant girl *en route* to Angers? Tramping with a companion, he catches her making love with a shepherd boy in some woods. The boy flees, the companion chases him, and Ménétra takes the girl, 'half by consent, half by force'. To us it sounds like rape. So does the episode in the workers' bedroom in the inn of Montpellier. Ménétra notices that an apprentice tailor travelling with a cutler is actually a girl in disguise. When the cutler spends a night away on a job, Ménétra takes over for him in bed, again 'half by force and the other by consent'. As several men sleep in the same room, the girl doesn't know whom to accuse the next morning. Among themselves the guys joke that 'only the Parisian could have pulled off that stunt' and they drive the couple off the premises with laughter.

Back in Paris, Ménétra seduces the wife of one of his best friends and the mistress of another. He covers up the first exploit, but the second leads to a fight and some curious philosophizing: 'That made me realize that jealousy is a sickness, that those who are stricken by it forget their best friends'. Ménétra claims to guide his own behaviour by a simpler precept: 'There is no pleasure where there is trouble.' But this popular hedonism undoes itself in one episode after another.

Consider our hero's triple triumph over old-man Pinard, a family friend from his neighbourhood in Paris. Pinard turns to Ménétra for advice: he cannot discipline his daughters, especially the older one who is having an affair with Ménétra's cousin and fellow man-about-town, Chenier. Ménétra uses the information to seduce the younger girl; then the mother, who is 'better value than her two daughters'; and finally the older girl, whom he wins by revealing that Chenier has taken up with a new mistress. Each of the Pinard women reports to Ménétra's room at her allotted hour. But the old man traces the traffic to its source. After a furious lecture about family honour, he challenges Ménétra to a fight with broomsticks. Ménétra smashes his wrist and leaves him on the battleground: a victory in combat, a belly laugh, and three more conquests added to the list.

We are meant to respond to these stories as Ménétra's mates did, with guffaws. But the jokes no longer work. It is not simply that we do not find cuckolds funny and women 'merchandise for man', as Ménétra puts it in his perfect phallocratic style. Story-telling assumes some complicity between raconteur and audience. It takes place on a common ground, where cues and responses are shared and a great deal can be said because a great deal goes without saying. Two centuries of the civilizing process have eroded that ground so badly that we no longer share much of it with Ménétra. His text is no longer straightforwardly funny. It is strange.

Its strangeness derives in part, from the way it works against itself. While presenting his life as one long romp through haystacks and boudoirs, Ménétra inadvertently turns up information that makes him look small, weak, and lonely – the very opposite of the he-man that he puts up front. If we rearrange the biographical details interspersed between the jokes, we see that Ménétra, like most Parisian babies, spent his first years with a wet-nurse outside the city. His mother died before he reached the age of two. When his father and grandmother came to visit him one day, they found him begging outside a church. The wet-nurse had taught him to imitate a deaf mute in order to pick up some extra pennies. He returned with his grandmother and lived with her until the age of eleven. Then he moved in with his father, who had acquired a new wife, and learned the glazier's craft. He also learned how to dodge blows and to sleep under the bridges of the Seine when his father became too violent.

The brutality increased as the boy turned into an adolescent and the father, widowed for the second time, took to drink. In one brawl, the old man broke young Jacques-Louis's jaw. In another, he dislocated a leg, and in a third the boy drew a knife. It was time to leave home. After returning from his *tour de France*, Ménétra married a girl with enough of a dowry to help him establish his own shop. And soon he was quarrelling with his own children, a boy and a girl, just as his father had quarrelled with him.

Ménétra narrates the whole cycle in a matter-of-fact way, without self-pity or guilt, but in doing so he undercuts the notion of life as a laugh. In the end, it transpires that he has been disowned by his father, betrayed by his comrades, deserted by his wife, and abandoned by his son, who ran off to another shop as soon as he learned the trade. What has become of all the women? we may ask; and we notice that Ménétra almost never mentions them by name, not even his wife. Although they make an impressive string of conquests, they are interchangeable, like the faceless nuns and farmers' daughters of the standard jokes. In looking back over them, Ménétra thinks of the glazier's widow he had left in Nîmes. She had offered him her heart as well as her bed. Had he been wrong to abandon her? he wonders. Had he missed something all along – namely, love? 'I knew love only as pleasure and not as perfect friendship.' When Ménétra reached the end of his life, he faced death as Don Giovanni did, alone. Perhaps ultimately the joke was on him.

The anxiety beneath the swagger in Ménétra's autobiography makes us feel that we have come in contact with a believable human being, someone like ourselves. But we do not close the book with a reassuring refrain, *homo sum*, ringing in our ears, because the strangeness of the narrative keeps getting in the way.

We are constantly brought up short against things we cannot fathom – everything from expressions beyond the range of our dictionaries (what is so insulting about saying 'bougie à l'huile' to a monk?) to behaviour outside the scope of our experience (why does Ménétra take such delight in stealing chickens from a Jew?).

We cannot even get most of Ménétra's jokes. What is so funny, we wonder, about the scene in Bayonne that seemed hilarious to him: half-naked prostitutes shut in an iron cage and ducked in a river? Where is the charm in the 'charming farce' that he encountered in Lyons: a nobleman rounds up all the hunchbacks of the city and forces them to share a meal while being served and serenaded by equally deformed townsmen? Why does Ménétra find it impossible to contain his laughter when his boss stumbles while carrying a load of glass panes above his head? 'As he wasn't wearing a wig, his head went right through the panes, and he was collared; the bits of glass tore into his neck; the slightest movement caused him excruciating pain . . . I couldn't prevent myself from bursting into laughter and telling him he should have worn a hat.'

Laughter does not echo unambiguously across the ages. When it reaches us from the distant past, it make us sense the gap between our ancestors and ourselves rather than our common humanity. Ménétra's jokes are usually cruel, and they often suggest that he expressed the brotherhood of man by the spoliation of woman. In a typical 'prank', he and his pal Gombeaut raped a girl whom they had found making love with her boyfriend in the woods outside Paris. Each of them took a turn while the other held the boyfriend at bay, using a sword that he had left by his breeches in the grass. This feat consummated a pact that the two friends had made over a bottle of wine a few days earlier. 'We are great friends, but we must become brothers', they declared. So they sold their silver shoe buckles and spent the proceeds on a night together with a whore.

It will not do to attribute such episodes to some depravity peculiar to Ménétra. We find similar incidents in unexpected places. In his *Confessions*, Rousseau recounts that he once shared a street girl with his pals Grimm and Klüpfel and that he and his friend Carrio rented a virgin from her mother in Venice, although they did not go so far as to deflower her. The cultural distance between high and low literature in the age of the Enlightenment was less than one might think. Rousseau and Ménétra walked the same streets and shared the same narrative ground. Rousseau's side of the street seems familiar today. But viewed from Ménétra's side, it looks strange and disturbing. Did an element of Don Juanism – the crude, guffawing, gang-raping kind – go into the eighteenth-century ideal of the brotherhood of man?

It may not be necessary to go that far in attempting to explain the strangeness of Ménétra's text, but the text cries out for explanation. We might, for example, attribute some of the womanizing to class conflict. By seducing above his station, Ménétra reversed the usual line of sexual exploitation, which led from the top down, as in the peasant-bashing *noblesse oblige* of Don Giovanni's campaign for Zerlina. Ménétra and his fellow workers specialized in cuckolding their bosses: that was the funniest joke of all. When he arrived in Auch, Ménétra transmitted some venereal disease to the wife of his 'bourgeois', as the workers called their master. She passed it on to her husband, who, thinking it had come from another source, took his problem to Ménétra. Our hero was as skilled in folk medicine as in the arts of love. So he cured the grateful couple and left town with the blessing of the bourgeois, who never suspected that he owed his disease to his doctor.

We also might explain Ménétra's pranks as variations on the theme of social and economic advancement. In the glazier's trade, as in many other skilled crafts, masterships were restricted in number and transmissible through widows. As the masters grew old and died, their widows took up with journeymen, who in turn took over the shops. Ménétra bragged that he could have fornicated his way to the top of many businesses on his *tour de France*. When one of his mates broke up with a master's wife, Ménétra took him to a tavern and consoled him with a proposition: 'I'll buy her from you for a bottle of wine and a salad'. After sharing the food and later the woman, they considered themselves 'brothers'.

That episode suggests another explanation: male bonding. The fellow travellers often expressed their fellowship by sharing women. They even felt united by venereal disease, which made them accomplices in a common dirty joke. After seducing a cook, Ménétra discovered that he had come down with a case of the clap that was also afflicting two of his drinking partners. Having traced it to the same source, they proclaimed laughingly that they, too, had become 'brothers'; and they toasted their fraternity in the tavern before undergoing a mercury treatment together. Perhaps a similar kind of complicity bound Leporello to Don Giovanni, despite the poor wages.

But whatever sociological gloss you apply to the text – class rivalry, social mobility, or peer group solidarity – it remains irreduceably strange. Ménétra lived in a world so saturated with violence and death that we can barely imagine it. We may have had some hard knocks in the subways of New York or the dark alleys of Soho, but how many of us encounter corpses on our daily rounds? Ménétra ran into them all the time, being fished out of the Seine, exposed on gibbets, and carted through the streets after fights and funerals. When he woke up one morning in a workers' inn, he found that his bedmate was dead. When his mate got up to urinate in another inn, he tripped over a corpse that had been stashed under the bed before their arrival.

Ménétra begins his life story by remarking casually that two of his three siblings died at their wet nurses – a common experience, according to the historical demographers. He goes on to relate all sorts of violent incidents. A friend blows off his nose while playing with firecrackers. Two others blind themselves. A cousin kills a scullery maid in the kitchen while toying with a pistol. A fellow worker, sotted with drink, falls asleep by the Pont Neuf and kills himself by tumbling into the Seine. Another drinking partner dies after downing a bottle of poison that he mistook for brandy. A woman in an apartment upstairs quarrels with her husband and jumps out the window, impaling herself on the wrought-iron sign of the shop below. The body count of the *Journal* is nearly as imposing as the toll of seductions.

Ménétra probably inflated it in the course of the story telling, but his rhetoric is significant in itself. It shows that he assumed familiarity with death on the part of his readers and that he drew on the macabre element in the popular culture of his time. For example, he relates the crimes of La Giroux, a notorious murderess, in the manner of the broadsides sold at her execution. He describes buying a broadside himself and then adds a characteristic touch: during her last moments he worried that she would inculpate him by revealing that he had had her maidenhead. Ménétra reports the crimes and punishment of the Duhamel gang in similar fashion, dwelling on the most sensational details. 'The monster Duhamel' had killed his mistress, grilled her heart, and eaten it. 'During his interrogation, he boldly said to the lieutenant-criminal of police, "Monsieur, if you had tasted it but once, you could never get enough".'

Ménétra's narrative is saturated with the ingredients of Parisian popular culture. Like most Parisians, he was fascinated with the public hangman, Henri Samson, who supposedly possessed extraordinary healing powers somehow related to his familiarity with death. At one point, when Ménétra fell into a strange torpor, 'Monsieur Henri' put him back on his feet by administering a potion brewed from the body of a freshly executed criminal.

But most of the potions consumed by Ménétra were white wines served with some roasted sparrow or salad in a tavern. The tavern, rather than the church, was the key institution in the culture of his craft. It provided a fraternal atmosphere for the ceremonies of the *compagnonnage*. Ménétra ate and drank his way through many rites of passage and even invented one of his own, a burlesque version of baptism and the Eucharist. It was such a hit, he claimed, that the leaders of the *compagnonnage* took it seriously and reprimanded him for flooding their association with schismatic 'journeymen of the crust'.

He also acted in earnest as a master of ceremonies. His production of the glaziers' feast of Saint Luke in Lyons seemed in retrospect to have been the high point of his life – rather as Don Giovanni seemed to reach the apogee of his career in the grand party he hosted at the end of Act One in the opera, though Ménétra staged festivities in a manner peculiar to the culture of his class. He had all the glaziers' shops hung with flowers and all the journeymen decked out in grey suits with white gloves and stockings, their hair curled and done up in white ribbons. They paraded through the streets carrying bouquets and the insignia of their craft to the sound of violins and oboes. Then, for nearly a week, they ate, drank, and danced themselves silly. The cost came to three hundred days' worth of labour, but they did not worry about it, because they did not calculate time and money as modern workers do. Instead, they valued excess – over-eating, heavy drinking, extravagant spending, profligate wenching, hard brawling, big talking, and belly laughing.

All these attitudes fit together in a plebeian culture that was essentially Rabelaisian. While the upper classes snickered over Voltaire or wept over Rousseau, the working men, and perhaps many of the women, elbowed and shouldered their way through a rowdy world that Rabelais had captured in writing two centuries earlier. Mikhail Bakhtin has shown that popular Rabelaisianism had a revolutionary edge to it. Could it have been the source of the ideology that Ménétra brought into the Revolution?

We cannot answer that question definitively, because Ménétra wrote only a short and garbled account of his experience as a sans-culotte. He saw the Terror at street level, where party lines disappeared in neighbourhood feuds and politics degenerated into *règlements de compte*. Robespierre and others do not appear in his narrative, but the people swarm through it – the common people, masters and journeymen alike – storming the Bastille, marching on the Tuileries Palace, departing to face the invading armies at the border. This popular revolution did not derive from the Enlightenment, but it realized some of the principles that Ménétra had assimilated under the Old Regime. We can hear the future sans-culotte in the orator who toasted his fellow glaziers at the feast of Saint Luke in Lyons: 'My friends, today we are all comrades together, and we all act in unison'.

Similar ideas can be found in the *Social Contract*. But to understand the way they resonated in the revolutionary sections of Paris, we need to go beyond Rousseau to Rabelais. Liberty and equality appear in *Gargantua* and *Pantagruel* as a festive throwing off of constraints and a sharing of the good things in life – something akin to what Ménétra meant by 'pleasure without trouble (*gêne*)' and to what the sans-culottes expressed as *liberté sans gêne* and *égalité dans les jouissances*.[4] Seen through Rabelais, Ménétra can help us grasp the third component of the sans-culotte trinity, the one that seems most mysterious today: fraternity. Ménétra did not learn brotherhood from books but from drinking and wenching with fellow travellers on a *tour de France*. His kind of fraternity could be violent and cruel, but in the supreme test of 1793–4 it united ordinary Frenchmen in a struggle not merely to fill the belly and rescue the republic but to save a way of life.

Because that way of life was transmitted on the road and in the tavern by men who did not write books, it has disappeared from history. Histories are composed of Enlightenment and Revolution, not the tales told by Ménétra. But once we have read those tales, the past assumes a different shape. By taking us into his story, Ménétra helps us share some common ground with the common man. It is an unsettling experience. The Enlightenment and the Revolution will never be the same. Nor will *Don Giovanni*.

Notes

1 Daniel Roche (ed.) *Journal de ma vie. Jacques-Louis Ménétra, Compagnon Vitrier au 18e siècle* (Paris, 1982). For background information about Ménétra and his text, see the essays by Roche that precede and follow it.

2 Alain Lottin, *Vie et mentalité d'un Lillois sous Louis XIV* (Lille, 1968); Giles Barber (ed.), *Nicolas Contat. Anecodotes typographiques* (Oxford, 1980); Jean-Marie Goulemot (ed.), Valentin Jamerey-Duval, *Mémoires* (Paris, 1981); and Emmanuel le Roy Ladurie and Orest Ranum (eds.), *Pierre Prion, scribe: mémoires d'un écrivain de campagne au XVIIIe siècle* (Paris, 1985).

3 See the material culled from the archives by Daniel Roche and cited in his introduction to the *Journal*, pp. 19–21.

4 The sans-culotte ideals are discussed at length in Albert Soboul, *Les Sans-Culottes parisiens en l'an II* (Paris, 1962). As an example of Ménétra's version, see *Journal de ma vie*, p. 198.

Donna Abbandonata

LAWRENCE LIPKING

'She sounds like a printed book!' Leporello comments in the second scene of *Don Giovanni*, after hearing Donna Elvira recite her grievances against her faithless lover. And indeed there is something formulaic, even glib, about this angry eloquence. We seem to have heard it all before. The cruel man has crept into her house, stolen her heart, called her his wife and then, after three days of love, abandoned her, fled, and left her to the remorse and tears that are her penalty for having loved him too well. Donna Elvira tells the story with feeling. She has probably told it too many times already, obsessively, like some ancient mariner, to whoever will listen. In fact this is her catalogue or card of identity: the credentials of an abandoned woman. And the list of complaints makes a perfect match with the libertine's list of conquests. In a moment she will have to attend and suffer while Leporello reads another catalogue from another book, the sum of seductions that reduces her unique sense of pain and betrayal to one among two thousand and sixty-four.

What book does Donna Elvira sound like? So many women in literature have shared her grievances that the possibilities seem as bottomless as Leporello's list. But many listeners in Mozart's day would have associated the story of an abandoned woman with one particular book, the *Lettres Portugaises* or *Letters of a Portuguese Nun* (1669). The popularity and influence of this little work can hardly be overestimated. In five brilliant letters (seven others survive in manuscript) 'Sister Mariana Alcoforado' cries out to the chevalier who has seduced and deserted her. One passion succeeds another: first fear and torment, then disgust, then a furious jealousy, then numbness, and finally contempt for the man who has proved so pathetically inferior to the idea of love that she carries within her. The chevalier did not respond. Yet generations of readers came to adore the nun, wept over her distress, and reverenced her letters as the most basic textbook of love.

She has appealed especially to such self-proclaimed experts on women as Stendhal and Rilke, who use Mariana as a key to unlock the secrets of feeling that women know instinctively and men always get wrong. They also pity her. The 'Poverina! Poverina!' that Don Giovanni murmurs beneath Donna Elvira's first aria has been echoed, doubtless with equal sincerity, by most readers of the *Portuguese Letters*. Such male sympathy should not be surprising, since the weight of scholarly opinion now attributes the letters to a male author, Gabriel de Lavergne de Guilleragues. The nun is a heroine after a man's heart. Her whole being depends on the man who has left her, the cause and only remedy of her anguish. Hence men find her easy to read. The words that flow from the mouth of Mariana or Donna Elvira are just what a man might imagine a woman would say when deprived of his presence. She would, of course, want him back. He knows her text by heart because he wrote it.

Yet Donna Elvira might have been echoing older books as well. Four years before the *Portuguese Letters*, for instance, Molière's *Dom Juan* had fashioned an Elvira quite similar to da Ponte's and Mozart's. Perhaps that character had helped shape the Portuguese Nun herself; or perhaps Mozart's Donna Elvira was reciting her own history from a prior edition. In any event, her case is far from unique. The majority of great heroines and prima donnas, in Western tradition, have been abandoned women. Even the word 'heroine' reflects that tradition. It derives from Ovid's *Heroides* or *Heroic Epistles*, the classic book in which fifteen famous women, from Penelope to Sappho, write letters of passion and despair to the men who have left them. Again and again the pattern is repeated: the lover stamps his image on the woman's heart and goes; she stays, pursues him with her thoughts, and gradually turns her sense of abandonment into a way of life. Ovid acknowledges no other kind of heroine.

The ingenuity of the *Heroides* consists in the number of variations it can play on this single theme. The poet retells the old myths and stories from the heroine's point of view, thus substituting Penelope's endurance or Dido's fury for the authorized male heroics of cunning Odysseus or pious Aeneas. The result is an anti-epic. No action ensues, no plot ever reaches an end. Instead, one love letter follows another, and each is full of tears (often streaking the ink). Not even Ovid's skill at varying the tone can ward off shades of monotony and claustrophobia. But many female authors, from Héloïse to Madame de Staël, constructed their own literary identities on this model of the heroine. There Donna Elvira could find her history printed.

It was only with the rise of the libertine, however, that the modern abandoned woman really came into her own. For the business of the libertine is precisely to make as many abandoned women as he can. In Rilke's poem 'Don Juan's Selection' (1908) the great lover is given his charge: to educate women into the deep truths of loneliness and solitude, thereby enabling them to 'surpass and outcry Héloïse'. He will do this by throwing them over. Love develops its ultimate purity in the absence of the beloved. Hence Rilke seems genuinely to have believed that when he abandoned women he did them a favour. At any rate, he points out the perverse logic that weds Don Giovanni to Donna Elvira, the perfect fit of the one who always leaves with the one who is always left. Whether or not they deserve each other, they do bring each other out. Don Giovanni stands revealed in his true colours, an embodiment of the masculine principle that cares for nothing but the exercise of dominating sexual power – 'barbaro', as Donna Elvira likes to call him. He is all man, all appetite; that is to say, all phallus. And Donna Elvira stands for all women, the stereotypical feminine principle or womb that wants to be filled and protected and loved and never lonely again. The two are as close – and as distinct – as pages in a book. Significantly, Leporello's phrase for Elvira's account of her betrayal – 'like a printed book!' – repeats the words that his counterpart, Molière's Sganarelle, had applied to Dom Juan's justification of his conquests. The libertine and the abandoned woman express themselves with an identical relentless fluency, by rote, without having to think. That is because their roles are so well established. Both are creatures of print who provide the grounds for each other, impeccably black and white.

Yet the woman's role is harder. Unlike Don Giovanni, whose lack of feeling for anyone else allows him to manipulate any situation, playing the charmer or bully by turns, Donna Elvira lives at her wit's end, tossing between extremities of passion – savage revenge and tenderness, the bounds of love and hate. She is never quite under control. Indeed, at times she seems to have wandered into *Don Giovanni* from some more primitive form of opera, a florid and static *opera seria* rather than *dramma giocoso*. Thus at her first entrance, without any warm-up, she launches into an amazing series of vocal leaps and bursts of rage: 'Who can tell me where that brute is? . . . I'll tear out his heart!' From the beginning Elvira lunges at notes as if they were her prey (a notorious pitfall for sopranos). Meanwhile the violins add their own commentary with jagged rhythms and accents. Such mania hovers on the brink of the absurd, and Mozart exploits the effect with music that approaches brilliant parody. The abandoned woman seems always to feel *too much*. Nor do we always know whether to cry or laugh.

To some extent this predicament derives from the word 'abandoned' itself. In Italian and other Romance languages as well as in English, the woman's 'abandon' suggests a basic ambiguity: She may be either forsaken or shameless, abandoned *by* or abandoned *to*. Even the etymology of the word yields the same double sense. The root contains 'power or control' (Late Latin *bandum*, cognate with English 'ban') modified by the preposition *ad* ('to') so as to stand equally for slavery or freedom, either the state of being in someone else's power or the state of an outlaw. An abandoned woman is the slave of her lover. Yet once exiled from his presence she has nothing left to lose and takes the reins into her own hands. Donna Elvira exemplifies this curious relation to power. On the one hand she is Don Giovanni's dupe or chattel, drawn magnetically after him and wilfully co-operating in her own deception. On the other, she acknowledges no authority but her own passion. Completely under the spell of the ideal lover she has half created, she can fail to recognize the real Don Giovanni when she sees him. Elvira is constantly carried away. Quite capable of sacrificing herself for her lover or hounding him to his death, abandoned both *by* and *to*, she lives in a world of her own. And there she makes her own laws.

The whole tradition of the abandoned heroine sustains a dual perspective toward her behaviour. Thus Ovid's collection of letters may be interpreted in contrary ways, as celebrating or satirizing the eternal feminine. To those who sympathize with heroines, the intensity of woman's love reveals the hollowness of the hero's life of bravery and shame and self-denial and emotional underdevelopment; if Aeneas had any sense he would stay with Dido. Yet those who admire the hero may think the heroine a shallow, self-involved romantic fool, someone who prefers sex to glory, and her own skin to the fate of empires; if Aeneas had stayed with Dido, there would have been no Rome or Latin for Ovid to write in. Over the shoulder of the scribbling woman, perhaps the poet smiles. Moreover, the heroine's protestations of deathless passion may smack of hypocrisy. According to La Rochefoucauld (a contemporary of the first Donna Elvira, the Portuguese Nun, and the Princess of Cleves), 'this mournful and tiresome vanity is generally found among ambitious women. Since their sex closes for them all roads that lead to glory, they struggle to gain celebrity by a show of inconsolable grief'. Not all readers have been so cynical. But abandoned women do make many people uneasy.

Perhaps that is their main function. By acting out the feelings that most of us are taught to conceal, they reproach the world for its collaboration with the games of seduction and power. Donna Elvira insists on prying behind closed doors. Nor does she consider any emotion too strong or shameful to express. Hysteria, carnality, self-loathing, infatuation, fury, abasement, longing – these are her daily bread. No wonder that genteel guests at a party would rather close their ears and go on dancing. But Donna Elvira's voice cannot be stilled; it threatens to bring down the house. She will not let the audience relax and enjoy Giovanni's

clever manœuvres, so impervious to anything deeper than pleasure. Instead her entrances tend to rupture the smooth progress of
the action and insert a note of anxiety or doubt. Breaking into the
final banquet scene, she does her best to interfere with Don
Giovanni's digestion; and when he triumphantly gloats over her
with his praise of women and wine – 'Sostegno e gloria/
D'umanità!' – she manages to have the last word: the screaming
'Ah!' that rhymes with his song but converts it to a new pitch of
horror and doom. Elvira is the first to recognize the approach of
hell; love has taught her how. And she is eager to pass her
knowledge on.

Unlike Giovanni himself, the audience listens. But probably
most of us are not quite sure how seriously to take Donna Elvira.
In the opera house interpretations range from melodrama to
farce. There are several reasons for this uncertainty, and each of
them is related to the ambiguity already glimpsed in the meaning
of 'abandoned'. First, one cannot ignore the element of sexual
display or titillation that bedevils any distracted heroine. Spell-
bound and self-absorbed, she exposes herself to the leers of
voyeurs on the stage as well as in the pit. Often she forgets to
adjust her dress. As Ariadne gazes after the flying Theseus, in
Catullus's definitive study of abandonment (Catullus 64, the
epyllion on Peleus and Thetis), her garments slip into the waves,
drawing our eyes over milky breasts and down to the feet. Similar
indignities are visited on Donna Elvira. Despite Leporello's
compassion for her infatuation, when given the chance to imper-
sonate Don Giovanni he cannot resist taking advantage, whether
with a caress or something more.

The woman forgets herself, the man's attention is pricked. Not
even Kierkegaard, in his visionary portrait of Elvira in *Either/Or*,
can help noticing her throbbing bosom and streaming hair; 'her
nun's veil was torn and floated out behind her, her thin white
gown would have betrayed much to a profane glance, had not the
passion in her countenance turned the attention of even the most
depraved of men upon itself.' That has the authentic note of a
male response to an abandoned woman: a deep respect for her
suffering that still manages to leave room for some speculative

glances behind the torn veil. Like Don Giovanni and his followers in the audience, Kierkegaard wants nothing more than to console her torment.

The *double entendre* that lurks in such phrases, however, refers not only to desire but to contempt for the woman who has lost control. Don Giovanni regards the opposite sex as essentially brainless, a lesser species on whom he has the right to operate. Even the proud and articulate Donna Elvira becomes a fool immediately when touched in the right place. The apparent success of Giovanni's assumptions about women may be a second reason for discomfort in the audience. If abandonment brings out the worst in women, their enslavement to men or to passion, it also brings out the worst in common attitudes toward women. From ancient times the treatment of abandoned women has reduced them to a few types or caricatures: the poor lost soul or avenging virago. In literature, theatre and opera the same sad choice recurs, as if the possibilities of heroinism were exhausted by a waif and a fury – Penelope and Clytemnestra, Cio-Cio-San and Katisha, Ophelia and Grendel's mother. Donna Elvira oscillates between those extremes. Fierce at one moment, melting the next, she dances like a puppet on a string, while Mozart's music misses no chance to remind us of her frailty. Even when most serious she is vulnerable to ridicule, as in the extraordinary trio early in Act Two, where her troubled, budding hope for reconciliation harmonizes with Giovanni's self-congratulation at deceiving her and Leporello's amazement at her credulity. The beauty of what we hear is almost (but not quite) enough to cover the embarrassment we feel at watching Elvira's foolishness exposed. Delicate and delicious as the scene may be, it also indulges in a smile at the sex-starved heroine's expense.

Indeed, Elvira's infatuation may be thought to amount not merely to weakness but madness. That is a third reason for our uncertainty about how to take her. Is she quite sane? Don Giovanni has some success in persuading the company that her accusations of him prove she is out of her mind; and from his point of view that diagnosis must look correct, since only a madwoman would make such a fuss about so insignificant an affair as the usual seduction and betrayal. We know better, of course. Yet Elvira's obsession, her extremity, her rapid shifts of mood – all perfectly realized not only by what she sings but by orchestral punctuation and italics – do indicate that she is on the edge of madness.

In the late eighteenth century, an age of sensibility, not many abandoned women escaped that fate. A vogue of mad scenes swept the stage, and heroines often adopted the mannerisms so well sketched by fifteen-year-old Jane Austen: 'My voice faltered, My Eyes assumed a vacant Stare, My face became as pale as Death, and my Senses were considerably impaired – . "Talk not to me of Phaetons (said I, raving in a frantic, incoherent manner) – Give me a violin – ." ' The description of symptoms here derives from Sappho's familiar Second Ode, a famous seizure of love.* But by Mozart's and Austen's time, in the wake of Werther, that lyric was regularly translated and interpreted as a longing for death, just as Sappho herself was transformed into 'Phaon's girl', a morbid, love-lorn depressive better known as a suicide than a poet.

Elvira follows the manic-depressive tradition. Bewitched by the phantom lover who has faded away like a dream, she summons up a feverish energy to hunt him down; but once he has gone she has no more to live for. Hence her final words, 'I'll go to a retreat to end my life', hint at an equivocation. Will she enter a convent to live out her days, or will she kill herself? Convention dictates the former. In the sources of *Don Giovanni* Elvira has come from a nunnery and will return there, though da Ponte carefully blurs the point. But Mozart's Elvira has death on her mind. 'I feel as if I were dying', she repeats during the sextet in Act Two, accompanied by a rising chromatic shudder in the strings; and though here as elsewhere she may be confusing erotic and literal 'dying' (as Daniel Heartz has argued), the apprehensions that usually darken the scene when she appears, like a *memento mori*. If we laugh at her extravagance, as Don Giovanni does, we laugh at our peril.

*'Phainetai moi' ('He seems to me a god'), Lobel-Page 31. Austen would have known the translation by Ambrose Philips.

Each entrance of Elvira takes the same form. Abandoned, wild, and manic-depressive, she stirs and then stifles our laughter. It is almost as if she were daring the audience to laugh. Such heroines turn the mood of the comedy inward, shifting the games of spectacle, movement, and pleasure to sombre sensations of pity and fear. The house becomes quiet. At moments like these, when silence hangs in the air like a collective, intimate brown study, there is always the danger of nervous coughing. And the mixture of self-recognition and restlessness affords a final reason for the disconcerting effect of Donna Elvira. Her feelings strike too close for comfort. Amidst the gaiety and bustle of the opera, which even murder hardly interrupts, she reminds each member of the audience of his or her own isolation. The abandoned woman communicates her sense of loss like an infection. Caught up in the action, each of us (whatever our moral disapproval) is in complicity with the facile, amusing stratagems of Don Giovanni. In this respect Leporello serves as our surrogate. He makes wry faces but he goes along with his master, and while condemning the libertine code he also enjoys it. Yet Donna Elvira will not let him or us get away with it. She shames us for giving in to the entertainment and warns us that when we go home we shall be alone with ourselves. Therefore we laugh at her; there is safety in numbers. Nevertheless, in the long run truth is on her side. Most of us know little about being heroes, about exercising power without conscience, debauching multitudes, and forcing the devil himself to take an interest in our doings. But most of us do know something about feeling lost and lonely. Donna Elvira speaks for those private feelings.

The relationship between the ways of the hero and the heroine, between his deliberate forgetfulness and her good memory, is at the heart of the opera. Other characters also have their moments, to be sure. No one will overlook the impenetrable fortitude of Donna Anna, or Zerlina's artful artlessness. Yet only Elvira has taken Giovanni's full measure. Despite her susceptibility to his wiles, she seems almost able to read his mind, as if prior carnal knowledge has enabled her to sniff out each of his movements. Whenever his appetite is about to be satisfied she arrives on the spot, fatally cramping his style. Perhaps this does not require much insight, since no one who always expects the worst from Don Giovanni is ever likely to be disappointed. But Elvira is more than a policewoman. She assumes the form of Giovanni's nemesis, his missing conscience, his alter ego. That is to say, she supplies what he lacks, the pity and fear that mark a human being.

In fact she is all too human. Few if any of Mozart's characters contradict themselves so often, changing in a moment or a phrase from implacable resentment to abject surrender. Music reveals these contrapuntal emotions with more precision and detail than words alone can manage, since much of the time her vocal line is interwoven with comments from the orchestra or other voices, like a running marginal gloss that points out inconsistencies in the text. We eavesdrop on Elvira's quandaries. Interestingly, her most direct presentation of this state ('Wretched Elvira, what contrary feelings batter your heart!'), the recitative and aria added for Vienna, seems least effective, because nothing is left to our imaginations and nothing in the accompaniment contradicts what she says. The heroine impresses us most when opposing strains in the music tear her apart. Such rending does not signify any lack of coherence in the character, of course, but rather Mozart's ability to catch her quick changes. Elvira's unsteady heartbeat, to which she calls attention with variations on the word 'palpitate', defines her special nature. She is strung up more tightly than others, she lives more intensely. Moreover, she understands her own pathology. The violence done to her illusions has brought her to a sort of posthumous existence, in which she is conscious of the futility of her hopes even while acting them out. Alone at the final curtain, she will have no future. The abandoned woman dwells on the ghosts of the past and conjures them into angry, feverish presence. By comparison most other characters seem one-dimensional.

Yet the opera does not belong to Donna Elvira. It is ruled by a libertine hero whose indifference to the past or to ordinary heartbreak approaches the superhuman. Structurally the abandoned woman is merely a foil for Don Giovanni. She testifies to his previous success, sets off his unregenerate nature, and expresses the anxiety he is not allowed to feel. Every plot requires a worthy antagonist or counter-plotter. Ultimately Donna Elvira exists in order to demonstrate the truth of Leporello's observation about his master: 'If not moved by her sorrow, he has a heart of stone or has no heart at all.' Just so. Contrasted with the full humanity of a passionate, fallible woman, the man shows what stuff he is made of. The stone guest will soon claim the stone heart.

Thus fate comes on cue for the man who has preyed upon women. But maybe that conclusion seems too pat. In spite of all the irresistible, pounding energy of Mozart's damnation scene, a liberated age is likely to think this heavenly overkill less suitable for grown-ups than for children. 'We all have seen him in the pantomime,' Byron remarks with casual unconcern at the beginning of his own *Don Juan*, 'Sent to the devil somewhat ere his time.' Many critics register the same detachment about *Don Giovanni*. Mozart has spent his genius on an outmoded moral relic, thrilling but not serious. The *deus ex machina* that winds up the action relies on make-up and trap-doors and fire that could not singe a sleeve. In real life the aristocrat would bribe the officials and go scot-free. Furthermore, the true moral of the story, as a libertine might see it, seems far from instructive: raping a daughter is permissible, so long as one does not also kill her father. Heaven favours the patriarch.

The role of Donna Elvira may hint, however, at a somewhat different moral. As we have seen, abandoned women and abandoning men seem made for each other – at least in literature. The hero demonstrates his heroism by giving the heroine up, suppressing his emotions as she succumbs to hers. The line that separates the two is as sharp as the gulf between female and male. But sometimes men and women cross that line. Feelings of abandonment afflict both sexes, and some psychologists would go so far as to maintain that the fear of being abandoned – whether by parents or lovers – is the primal fear for men as well as women. The misfortunes of Oedipus stem from his being abandoned. Thus even the libertine may be viewed as in flight not so much from a woman as from an image of himself as a possible loser, the one who might be left. Don Giovanni abandons Donna Elvira before she can abandon him, and denies that any speck of her humanity can cling to his flesh. It is impossible to imagine that he could ever shed a single honest tear; he leaves all feelings behind. This might be considered his triumph. Yet it also might be seen as his punishment.

Indeed, the shadow that follows Donna Elvira turns out to be stronger than Don Giovanni's bravado. The opera witnesses his growing isolation, his shrivelling to lonely defiance. At the close of the first Act a crowd surrounds the hero; as the second Act nears its climax his bluster cannot disguise the fact that a man with so many names on his list is dining alone, or throwing a party to which nobody comes – except the one guest he would rather not see. The numbers dwindle to one. 'I myself am hell;/ nobody's here – ' Don Giovanni never admits a moment of fear, nor would he concede that Donna Elvira might be his other self. But in the end, no matter how many he has abandoned, abandonment will come to visit him. At last he has the partner he deserves.

The Seductions of Women

JANE MILLER

Operas have to seduce us. When they fail to we all too easily see
through to the fumbling flasher, abjectly exposing his tricks and
plans for our enchantment, embarrassingly resistible. Don Giovanni himself must be irresistible, certain to notch us all up.
Murderer, bandit, burglar he may be, but to see through his
seductions, to deny him ourselves, is to spoil the fun, his fun, our
fun, the complicity of the won-over audience. Seductions can
seem to have equivalent meanings for women as for men in such a
scenario. A woman, after all, may 'let herself be seduced' or even,
Delilah-like, seduce. She may also, a Zerlina, resist, her evasions
read as confirming, titillating, encouraging, or as the attractive
face of a hard-nosed peasant economic sense. Most kinds of
resistance will be accommodated already, and explained, within
the desires and the achievements of the seducer. What women
may not do is cancel the seduction, deny its nature, rename it,
separating and distancing themselves from its intentions and its
fulfilment. To do that is not just to misname but shamefully to
over-react. Yet it is possible to construe women's inclusion as
willing participants in their own seduction as a sleight-of-hand
disguising their exclusion from the language which performs it.
Seduction contains and measures out women's incapacity to speak
for themselves or to claim as unadulterated a sexuality independent of men's dreams of them. If women's testimony is assumed,
written in, to the act of seduction itself, their interrogation of the
act, like their interrogation of the narrative which announces that
act, will be short-circuited and disallowed.

It is important to pornography, in its least exalted forms as in its most, for women to participate excitedly in their own and in other women's seduction. Moreover, accounts of seduction and of women's role as procurers of it, aiders and abetters of it, which purport to be written by women when they are not, are also common features of the genre. It is not merely that myths and legends of the *Don Giovanni* kind tell stories which place women anomalously in relation to men's designs on them, but that women who read such tales, or write them, are cast as androgynous, duplicitous and at fault. That casting is inevitable, perhaps, within stories which are intended to explain male sexuality, even to console men for its pains and confusions. The problems of all that for women are, as usual, multiple. For if seduction is stealthy and stolen it is also, necessarily, seductive and delightful, so that women are required to concede above all that seduction is quite different from rape, that they have wanted it and that their complicity has, more often than not, had dire consequences for men.

Foucault, who taught us to think about sexuality in terms of historical discourses and their relation to power, contributed, nonetheless, to a tradition which offered the libertine as a kind of libertarian, hero, free spirit and individualist. That tradition focused on women only in so far as they were the generalized object of male desire; thus narrowly determining women's scope for choice and resistance within narratives of seduction and ignoring the account of events they might have given themselves, if asked. The same tradition bypasses women as readers of such narratives, though they are readers who might, after all, be in a position either to endorse or deny them, or even to replace them with alternatives. If women readers are assumed or implied at all they must be presumed to switch allegiance effortlessly and often, from a man's view of it all to a receptive and womanly one. Such a woman would need to read a novel like *Les Liaisons dangereuses* through eyes which were not just male, but mistily misogynous, so that women become for women creatures who are variously complicit with men, either as predators or as willing, foolish or hypocritical prey.

It has above all been difficult for women to write of seduction and of seductive men and seducers within a tradition which has measured the seducer's claim to general sympathy or disapproval in terms of his stealing another man's property and thereby contravening civil law, divine law, or both. Women will have had other ways of considering that theft of themselves (and it will not always have seemed to be out of the frying pan and into the fire), but they will also have needed to contend with testimonies to their complicity in male versions, which have covered their tracks in mimicry and ventriloquism.

It is necessary to unravel actual women's stories of seduction from the falsetto productions of men, as a first step towards challenging those accounts of sexual relations and sexual differences which have established them as natural, universal, even eternal relations and differences, when they are always in fact historically specific and are, moreover, controlled as practice and as discourse by men, in their own interests. A powerful convention within such discourse is the attribution to women of views which men need women to have. Byron, for example, consoles his Don Juan with a letter from Donna Julia containing this stanza:

Man's love is of man's life a thing apart,
   'Tis woman's whole existence; man may range
The court, camp, church, the vessel, and the mart;
   Sword, gown, gain, glory, offer in exchange
Pride, fame, ambition, to fill up his heart,
   And few there are whom these cannot estrange;
Men have all these resources, we but one,
   To love again, and be again undone.

It is worth remembering that those famous lines were attributed by a famous seducer to a woman who has let herself be seduced away from her husband by the guileless and adolescent Don Juan. It is written from the convent in which, as an adulteress and a sinner, Donna Julia is complacently ready to spend the rest of her days. Men have wanted and needed to hear women tell them, as Byron gets Donna Julia to, that it is all right for men to love them and leave them, for how else would the world's business – whatever that might be for a Don Juan – get done?

In considering two novels about seducers, Samuel Richardson's *Clarissa* (1748-9) and Jane Austen's *Sense and Sensibility* (1811), I want to chart continuities and overlaps as well as gaps and discrepancies between them. For if the novels are separated by more than fifty years and by the sex and class of their authors they also have a good deal in common. It is possible, anyway, to see Jane Austen's novel as one in a kind of sequence, which might include novels as different as Fanny Burney's *Evelina* (1778) and George Eliot's *Adam Bede* (1859), novels by women which attempt to rewrite the seduction story, perhaps even *Clarissa* itself, from within its constraints. Those constraints involve women in collusion with their attackers and allow only so much resistance to assaults on their bodies and their integrity as consorts at all probably with their retaining their appeal for men.

Because Richardson made Clarissa a tireless writer, on whose version of events we are encouraged to rely, the novel has sometimes been read as championing women and deploring men. Readers of both sexes have certainly found it hard to resist the novel's seductions, for it is subtle and humorous and it tells us in marvellous detail and at extraordinary length about eighteenth-century life and gentlemen's treatment of women. And yet at the heart of this beguiling story is a rape. It is from Lovelace himself that we first learn of his raping Clarissa. It is an event he reports on with brief evasive elegance in letters to his friend, John Belford,

And thus, between terror, and the late hour, and what followed, she was diverted from the thoughts of getting out of the house to Mrs Leeson's, or anywhere else,

and then

And now, Belford, I can go no farther. The affair is over. Clarissa lives. And I am

Your humble servant,

R. LOVELACE

Lest that laconic allusion to a savage act be thought to stand straightforwardly for the value a reader might be expected, either by Lovelace or by Richardson himself, to put on it, those lines need some context and explaining. Clarissa herself could be said to be spared her own rape in the sense that she is first drugged and then shocked into unconsciousness. She remains in a coma, it turns out, for a week. It is necessary to the rest of the novel that she be beyond charges of either complicity or resistance at the time of the rape and that she be disqualified even as a witness to it. Clarissa must remain uncontaminated by the passions and the covetousness she inspires and provokes. Richardson has made of Clarissa a paragon and a saint, whose death in her nineteenth year and a white satin nightdress is hardly less than an apotheosis. She has been coveted by men from her childhood. She is favoured as heiress to her grandfather, pet of her unmarried uncles, valued by brother and father for her services as precocious housekeeper. She is also a clever businesswoman, expert in matters of law and wills and property, indefatigably given to improving herself, flawlessly beautiful, a devout Christian, a gifted linguist (more anxious to write French than to speak it) and an accomplished needlewoman, who is not above coining somewhat elaborate maxims of the sort: 'a woman who neglects the *useful* and the *elegant*, which distinguish *her own sex*, for the sake of obtaining the learning which is supposed more peculiar to the *other*, incurs more *contempt* by what she *foregoes* than she gains *credit* by what she *acquires*.' As John Stuart Mill put it, 'we are perpetually told that women are better than men, by those who are totally opposed to treating them as if they were as good.' This woman is not only better than men, she is far, far better than all the women in the novel too. Clarissa's mother and sister speedily and enthusiastically join in the general condemnation of Clarissa and leave her to Lovelace and his stratagems, while Clarissa's 'dear Miss Howe' answers her letters with dispatch but moves not a finger to visit her beleaguered friend. Clarissa is so idealized a man's woman that a woman reader may be forgiven for wondering whether she can be read as a woman at all.

Mrs Sinclair, the brothel keeper, who attends Lovelace and incarcerates Clarissa for him, is also meant as a woman. She is a creature of brutish vivacity, who is implicated in Clarissa's rape and in the novel's diffuse and violent antagonisms towards women. In a letter to Belford, just preceding his admission of rape, Lovelace offers this decription of Mrs Sinclair:

> The old dragon straddled up to her, with her arms kemboed again – her eyebrows erect, like the bristles upon a hog's back and, scowling over her shortened nose, more than half-hid her ferret eyes. Her mouth was distorted. She pouted out her blubber-lips, as if to bellows up wind and sputter into her horse-nostrils; and her chin was curdled, and more than usually prominent with passion.

That image is produced by Lovelace as he contemplates admitting to the rape he has committed. It may also be understood as in some sense filtered through the drugged and terrified perceptions of the helpless Clarissa. Its association with the rape and with Lovelace's urbane and only direct allusion to the rape chimes with some of the novel's central dilemmas.

The elements of that image of Mrs Sinclair are wilfully fragmented and overlaid. A composite monster, dragon, hog, ferret and horse, is distorted and curdled as it straddles and sputters. The strangeness of similar vocabulary is remarked on much later in the novel by Clarissa, who characterizes as 'female words' 'battered' and 'flurries' and suggests that 'all female words, though we are not sure of their derivation, have very significant meanings'. They are meanings, one must suppose, having something in common with the grunt and the snort and they appear in passages of menacing violence. At all events, we have here a strangely imagined and fabricated beast, predatory, indefinite and protean, which is also its own victim. This Beast could be said to consume its own Beauty. Ferocity is cornered, the hunter is caught, and the stench of fear, of cruelty and revenge, are carried equivocally by the passage, which is so curiously overblown and overwrought that it seems dispersed by the hatred which informs it.

It is an image which may be read as the expression of Lovelace's inadmissible terror of female sexuality, seen here as rampant, untamed, unmastered. Like the words of Dryden, which Lovelace quotes as explanation of his behaviour, 'with revenge it glows'. The rape which is so bizarrely absent from the text itself has been displaced by the hatred it was intended both to express and discipline. Mrs Sinclair, become monstrous, contains Lovelace's guilt and assuages it. She stands for his violent designs on women and for his rake's predilections and habits. His wry 'are not all rakes sad fellows?' is scuppered by that snorting beast who is a woman and therefore a justification for those habits, their victim, but also the nightmarish embodiment of the need in Lovelace to believe in the complicity of women. Richardson has him repeatedly resorting to that seducer's rhetoric, in which 'every woman is a rake in her heart . . . for *no wickedness is comparable to the wickedness of a woman*'.

Lovelace is, as he puts it to Belford, 'a notorious woman-eater'. The association of seduction with the hunting, the preparing and the eating of food is explicit and emphatic in the novel and is, of course, central to the value put on women and to the options open to Clarissa herself. She has learned from her brother that 'daughters are chickens brought up for the tables of other men'. At the beginning of the novel Clarissa herself is not only possessed of 'delicacy', but is delectable and is also responsible for her father's larder and his table. By the time of her self-induced and anorexic death she is described as 'iced', of spun-sugar frailty, a proper dessert. Yet for Lovelace women are also wild game, free for the taking and no man's property, there to be shot at, snared, trapped, surprised and netted. In this vein his language is closer to a hunter's than an eater's, for, as he points out, 'Does not the keen foxhunter endanger his neck and his bones in pursuit of a vermin which, when killed, is neither fit food for men nor dogs?' The reformed rake Belford reminds Lovelace that women caught 'unprepared for being seen' are filthy, diseased creatures. Birds must be speedily drawn and plucked and cooked. Clarissa's death, for which she has so exquisitely and seductively prepared herself, is preceded by Mrs Sinclair's.

> Her misfortune has not at all sunk but rather, as I thought, increased her flesh; rage and violence perhaps swelling her muscly features. Behold her then, spreading the whole tumbled bed with her huge quaggy carcase: her mill-post arms held up, her broad hands clenched with violence; her big eyes goggling and flaming-red as we may suppose those of a salamander; her matted grizzly hair made irreverend by her wickedness (her clouted head-dress being half off) spread about her fat ears and brawny neck; her livid lips parched, and working violently; her broad chin in convulsive motion; her wide mouth by reason of the contraction of her forehead (which seemed to be half-lost in its own frightful furrows) splitting her face, as it were, into two parts; and her huge tongue hideously rolling in it; heaving, puffing as if for breath, her bellows-shaped and various-coloured breasts ascending by turns to her chin and descending out of sight with the violence of her gaspings.

How infinitely preferable will be Clarissa's 'lovely corpse', dressed for the grave rather than the cauldron.

Richardson has done more than give Lovelace the best lines and all the jokes in *Clarissa*. His novel sympathetically enacts the compulsions and the contradictions of this self-hating and misogynous seducer by incorporating the mutinous independence and those other forms of resistance in Clarissa which are so expertly designed to keep alive Lovelace's interest in her. Initially, the novel's plot could be said to hinge on the consequences of Clarissa's split-second and probably quixotic decision to seek help from Lovelace in escaping her family and their plans to marry her to the unprepossessing Solmes. Thereafter, the novel's remarkable suspense and excitement are maintained – as

Lovelace's interest is maintained – through Clarissa's increasing provocations.

The novel itself, seducer-like, lovingly, gloatingly, lubriciously watches a young woman recoil from the unbearable encroachments of a threatening man and into the progressive divesting of that very physicality in herself which has inspired both lust and vengeance in her tormentor. Anorexia, illness, death become in the novel simultaneously a means of escape and the aphrodisiac ruses of a complicitous woman. As Clarissa works to concentrate her entire bodily existence into vapour, spirit, an early death, she is also congratulated implicitly for affording Lovelace the most intense sexual and emotional experience of his life. Clarissa's apotheosis is also Richardson's way of controlling his heroine, mastering her and bringing her to heel. Dying and dead she is 'prepared for being seen', totally possessed, seemly, contained within the pages of the novel, a man's woman. Had she followed the advice of her family and friends she might have redeemed the situation for herself by marrying her abductor, her seducer. Lovelace himself has prefigured the kind of triumph that would have been for Clarissa, and the kind of humiliation it would have spelled out for him: 'To be *despised by a* WIFE! – What a thought is that!'

Guardedness, a withholding of favours and a judicious coolness are the least of what is enjoined on young women in novels where seducers prowl. Clarissa's preparation for her death, her purchase of her own coffin and her use of it as a bedside writing table may be said to constitute the last word in guardedness: and as double-edged a weapon against Lovelace as it is meant to be, since it simultaneously excites his lust and protects her from it. In *Sense and Sensibility* it is precisely Marianne's 'Romantic' conviction that guardedness is squalid and that only the strongest emotions are worth either having or expressing which so alarms her sister Elinor on her behalf. Marianne's openness and generosity with the enchantingly handsome Willoughby go with preferring Scott to Pope and crooked trees to straight ones. In a novel which begins and ends with money and with the particular economics of women's dependence on fathers and husbands and brothers within the poorer sections of the early nineteenth-century gentry such behaviour in a beautiful sixteen-year-old girl is seen as inviting abuse. At this rate she will end up poor as well as miserable. Would Elinor regard her sister as less culpable, more virtuous, if she kept dalliance and money apart, as Willoughby does? In this as in much else Jane Austen expects higher standards of women than of men. Seducers are hazards which sensible young women must learn to detect and avoid.

Willoughby's first appearance, with his dogs and his gun, establishes him as a gentleman. Elinor, as enthusiastically as Marianne and Mrs Dashwood, responds at once to his beauty, his voice, his frank and graceful manners. The Dashwoods are relieved to learn that he is due to inherit from a rich old lady and that he has already a small estate of his own. Even at the point when he rushes back to London, leaving Marianne in tears and everyone in confusion as to his intentions towards her, Elinor is able to say to her mother, 'I love Willoughby, sincerely love him; and suspicion of his integrity cannot be more painful to yourself than to me'. And yet Willoughby is not just seductive, he is a seducer. It is not only, of course – as he later reveals – that his intentions towards Marianne have not been honourable, but that he has seduced Colonel Brandon's fifteen-year-old ward and abandoned her with a child. It is this act which makes Willoughby a serious seducer and which is at the centre of the novel's ambiguous treatment of the subject. It is an act which is condemned particularly as one 'which no man who can feel for another would do'. Marianne's mother will later be certain that her daughter could not have been happy 'with a man of libertine practices! With one who had so injured the peace of the dearest of our friends, and the best of men'. It is easy to feel that both these remarks register the injury to Colonel Brandon as more serious than the injuries done either to his ward or to Marianne. It is significant too that it takes a man to detect the bounder in another man.

Jane Austen's novels are principally concerned with the lives and the possibilities of women, even with very young women and the brief adventures they may embark on during what we would describe as their teenage or adolescent years, which will perhaps lead to marriage, and will end there. *Sense and Sensibility* does not, as *Clarissa* does, concern itself with the hunt, with the ways in which a libertine's appetite may wax and wane or be systematically maintained or increased. Indeed the seducer's motives are only of interest in so far as they might be able to provide some comfort to the young women who have been deceived and abandoned or who may feel they have been made fools of by him. Yet Jane Austen was also writing within a tradition which saw the seducer, provided he was also a gentleman, as a kind of sportsman. Young women had only themselves to blame if they let themselves get caught. We are, of course, meant to find absurd the words of Marianne's brother when he first sees her again after her disappointment with Willoughby. Yet their absurdity lies chiefly in their being uttered so blatantly and insensitively. They express quite recognizable anxieties.

At her time of life, anything of an illness destroys the bloom for ever! Hers has been a very short one! She was as handsome a girl last September as any I ever saw, and as likely to attract the men. There was something in her style of beauty to please them particularly. I remember Fanny used to say that she would marry sooner and better than you did: not but what she is exceedingly fond of *you* – but so it happened to strike her. She will be mistaken, however. I question whether Marianne *now* will marry a man worth more than five or six hundred a year at the utmost, and I am very much deceived if *you* do not do better.

The male tradition of seduction narratives focuses on female sexuality as a valuable commodity, worth a certain amount of money on the open market. It is a commodity owned by men and prized. The seducer of women disrupts the ordinary process of bargaining and exchange: intruding on the transaction by recognizing and appealing to the woman herself and to her sexual nature. If a seducer steals a woman from another man he will necessarily be seen to be doing so with the woman's consent (for otherwise it would be rape). That consent will justify the controlling of women by men, since it will demonstrate once again that women are sexually unbridled as well as undiscriminating. Jane Austen has made Marianne fatherless and outside her brother's direct financial control. To this extent she breaks with the tradition which makes the seducer's crime primarily an offence against a man. Yet Willoughby's seduction of Colonel Brandon's ward and his success with the woman the Colonel loves and wants to marry mark out the extent to which Jane Austen accepts a male account of it all. Her dilemma lay in reconciling this male view of Willoughby's transgression with her almost maternal need to believe some good of him, to make him credibly seductive, likeable, loveable and a young man of quite a different sort from Lovelace, one whom an intelligent young woman, if a rash one, might plausibly trust as well as love.

At the end of the novel, when Marianne seems after all likely to recover from what was nearly a fatal illness, exacerbated at the very least by Willoughby's betrayal of her, Willoughby himself appears. His attempts to gain Elinor's sympathy through elaborately alternating passages of self-exculpation, self-pity and abject apology work on the clear-headed and upright Elinor as a kind of seduction. He knows, and plays on, Elinor's passionate wish to have been mistaken about him. She is gratified to learn from him that he was and still is attached to Marianne and that he regrets his marriage. She takes in her stride his tales of debts, the reasons for them and even the view that they made marriage to any woman without a fortune of her own out of the question. Though she is occasionally stern she is also won over, even by his callous account of his treatment of Colonel Brandon's ward,

> I acknowledge that her situation and her character ought to have been respected by me. I do not mean to justify myself, but at the same time cannot leave you to suppose that I have nothing to urge, – that because she was injured, she was irreproachable, – and because I was a libertine, she must be a saint. If the violence of her passion, the weakness of her understanding – I do not mean, however, to defend myself.

Her affection for me deserved better treatment, and I often, with great self-reproach, recall the tenderness which, for a very short time, had the power of creating any return.

Elinor will remember him after their conversation as 'poor Willoughby', will allow herself a rudimentary wish that he might one day become a widower and available for remarriage and will often feel a 'pang' for him, a pang which is not on her sister's behalf alone.

Willoughby – he whom only half an hour ago she had abhorred as the most worthless of men – Willoughby, in spite of all his faults, excited a degree of commiseration for the sufferings produced by them, which made her think of him as now separated for ever from her family with a tenderness, a regret, rather in proportion, as she soon acknowledged within herself, to his wishes than to his merits.

The novel has laughed in the end at passionate love and at romance and has come down in favour of moderation and of young men and women marrying sensibly and with an eye to comfort and economic security. The excesses of *Clarissa* have been frowned on.

Stories and novels are bent, like operas, on seduction. They are out to cajole complicity from readers imagined in postures of mutinous independence. So long as the narrative of male seduction ignores the woman as its reader, or at best assumes her to be androgynous, the text will have closed in on itself, protecting its embalmed view of men's and women's libido, as *Clarissa* does, by identifying an independent sexuality in women – their refusal of the seducer – with the chaste and the corpse-like. Jane Austen was writing from within that tradition. She was constrained, as women writers have been, and still are in most cases, by the defeats that tradition predicts for women. *Sense and Sensibility* can be read, however, as challenging *Clarissa* and any account of seduction which settles for women being beasts, fools or dead. Jane Austen allows that women may find men seductive. She also emphatically requires of women that they take responsibility for their sexual natures. She certainly expected them to survive their errors and humiliations. Most importantly, she asserts the possibility of a woman's morality and a woman's resistance, even as she adumbrates the tradition which has made both so necessary and so difficult to represent.

Odzooks! A Man of Stone

Earth, heaven and hell in
eighteenth-century tomb sculpture

MALCOLM BAKER

O statua gentilissima,
Benchè di marmo siate . . .
(*Don Giovanni* Act II Scene 3)

When Leporello addresses the statue of the Commendatore in the cemetery and the marble figure responds, Mozart and da Ponte were bringing into play a contemporary public's perception of the ambivalent nature of sculpture. The statue, though stone, has the form and volume of a living man and appears to inhabit the same space as the spectator. This notion of a sculpture so deceptively realistic that it appeared to come alive was already established in the classical myth of Pygmalion and underlies the many medieval accounts of miracles in which statues of the Virgin and saints speak or gesture to the devout observer; by the eighteenth century the idea had become a commonplace of critical discourse concerning sculpture, whether in the form of a scholarly treatise or a newspaper report. It lies behind, for example, the reaction of the unsophisticated visitor from the country who comes across Roubiliac's statue of Handel in Vauxhall Gardens, as described in the *Gentleman's Magazine* in August 1742.

As still amaz'd I'm straying
O'er this enchanted grove,
I spy a Harper playing
All in his proud alcove.

Odzooks! A Man of Stone

I doff my hat, desiring
He'd tune up Buxom Joan
But what was I admiring
Odzooks! A man of stone.

If prompted by the contemplation of the figures on a tomb –
especially images of the recently deceased – this response
becomes far more potent and complex.

When a sculpture on a monument is perceived as a 'living
likeness', the spectator becomes uncertain about the boundary
between this world and the next. The earthly and other-wordly
are here juxtaposed and even mingled so that we, like Leporello,
are unsure whether the figure is intended to be dead or not. The
relationship between these two worlds forms the theme of much
eighteenth-century tomb imagery and it is against the background
of contemporary monument conventions and the assumptions
made by contemporary observers that the statue scene may be
best understood.

The variety of types of tomb sculpture produced in the
eighteenth century make any coherent classification difficult and
to use a handful of examples as the basis for generalizations about
changing attitudes to death throughout Europe would be mislead-
ing. The nature, scale and numbers of such memorials differ
markedly from one country to another. In France, monuments,
other than quite modest tablets, were normally commissioned by
figures of high rank, the most impressive being for royalty or
military heroes, while in England monuments of considerable
pretension were erected in small village churches not only for
minor noblemen but also for untitled gentlemen and bourgeois
merchants. In Germany monuments of any size are, by contrast,
relatively few, even for members of the nobility. Nevertheless,
despite these differences and the theological distinction in the
thinking of Protestant as opposed to Catholic patrons, many of
the same images were employed on monuments in widely
separated places. The combinations in which these were used,
however, indicate an ambiguity about death and the expectations
of an afterlife.

In a period in which the tenets of Christianity were being challenged by philosophical scepticism, commonly held beliefs included evangelical enthusiasms, deism and even atheism. Such positions determined attitudes to the relationship between this life and the next, and indeed to death itself. The way in which the relationship between these three elements was understood determined the nature of the imagery used on a tomb.

The earthly component of such monuments consists of the deceased's achievements and status in this world, expressed in the form of an epitaph, personification or sometimes a narrative scene. Prominent on the monuments to both Bishop Morosini (pl. 1) and Count Mitrowicz (pl. 2) is the figure of Fame, recording the distinctions and quality of the persons commemorated. The text of such epitaphs and the exact interpretation of the various personifications were discussed in detail in contemporary publications and occasioned much correspondence and public debate. It was recognized that one of the functions of such monuments was to celebrate the achievements of the great, and the French sculptor, Falconet, considered his prime duty was 'to perpetrate the memory of illustrious men'. The role of tomb sculpture is equally clearly stated in a commentary on Vinache's model for the monument to Cardinal Fleury, shown in the Paris Salon of 1743:

> Since the purpose of tombs is to make known to posterity the good qualities of those for whom they are erected, the sculptor should choose the most interesting moments in the life of his subject, those by which he has shown himself to best advantage.

The creation of monuments as celebrations of earthly glory had earlier been acknowledged in a sermon by the late seventeenth-century French theologian Bossuet but he contrasts this with the physical reality of death:

> When I consider the splendid tombs in which the great of this earth seem to be trying to hide the shame of their corruption, I

Monument to Bishop Francesco Morosini (died 1678) by Filippo Parodi (1630–1702) Santa Nicola dei Tolentini, Venice.

Using the rich visual effects of the late baroque, Parodi shows the Venetian patriarch looking heavenwards while the figure of Time lies defeated below the sarcophagus. Set against a backdrop of drapery, held by an angel, this dramatic scene expresses the antithesis between earthly time and the eternal. The personifications of Fame and Charity allude to the bishop's earthly qualities and achievements.

*Monument to Wenzel, Count Wratislaw von Mitrowicz (died 1712),
engraved in J. B. Fischer von Erlach's* Entwurff einer historischen
Architectur *(1721). Designed by Fischer von Erlach and carved by
Ferdinand Maximilian Brokoff. Erected 1714–16, St James, Prague.*

The pyramid, on which Fame records the titles of the deceased Chancel-
lor of Bohemia, was understood to endure until the end of time but is
here shown crumbling as von Mitrowicz is crowned by Divine Love.
Below are Time and the mourning figure of History.

The corruption of the Body, wax relief by Gaetano Giulio Zummo (1656–1701). Made about 1691–5.

A conventional image of a tomb with a female personification is here placed in the context of physical decay and decomposition. This was one of the wax groups described by many eighteenth-century visitors to Florence and which inspired the account in the Marquis de Sade's *Juliette* of 'a sepulchre filled with cadavers in which one could observe all the different stages of decomposition from the moment of death until the total destruction of individuality. This grim work of art was made of wax that was coloured so naturally that Nature herself could not have been more expressive or more real.'

Two syphilitic figures, wax by Gaetano Guilio Zummo (1656–1701). Made about 1691–5. Private collection, Florence.

These figures originally formed part of a large group, illustrating the effects of syphilis; this was made for Cosimo III whose son-in-law, the Elector of Bavaria, had contracted the disease.

Monument to Arminius Maurice, Maréchal de Saxe (1696–1750) by Jean-Baptiste Pigalle (1714–1785). Designed 1754–6 and completed in 1777.

One of the most celebrated and discussed of French eighteenth-century monuments, the Saxe tomb was explained in detail by the sculptor. Describing the animals to the general's left as symbols of the countries he defeated in battle, he turns to the central dramatic confrontation between Saxe and Death 'who with one hand opens the stone of the tomb and with the other holds the hourglass, which he shows to the general to indicate that his hour had come'. The general looks at Death 'proudly and with fearlessness descends to the tomb', while between them, France 'by the signs of grief, fear and despair on her face seems to wish Death to relent'.

Monument to Daniel Gottlieb Männlich (died 1701) and his wife by Andreas Schlüter (1659–1714). Designed in 1700, following the death of Männlich's wife. Bodemuseum, East Berlin; formerly in St Nicholas, Berlin.

The door of death had long symbolized the transition between this world and the next and here has a real function in the entrance to a family mausoleum. The married couple commemorated by the monument are shown in the conventional medallion form on the urn, but the composition is dominated by the dramatic scene of Death grasping the child above. Inspired by Holbein's early sixteenth-century print of the Dance of Death, the particularly forceful imagery may also allude to the death of the sculptor's own son in the same year.

Monument to Joseph Nightingale (died 1752) and Elizabeth, Lady Nightingale (died 1731) by Louis Francois Roubiliac (1702–1762). Designed 1758 and erected 1761. Westminster Abbey, London.

Although a monument to both husband and wife, the action shows Lady Nightingale, who died in childbirth, about to be attacked by Death, who has one foot still in the sarcophagus that may be seen behind the door of the tomb. Some of the imagery used here – the door and the skeleton, for example – is common to tomb sculpture throughout Europe from the mid-seventeenth-century onwards. But the preoccupation with death in contemporary English literature suggests that the skeletal personification here would be seen not merely as threatening but as a means of deliverance from the cares of this world to eternal life.

Monument to Maria Magdalena Langhans (died 1751) by Johann August Nahl (1710–1781). Completed 1751. Hindelbank, near Berne, Switzerland.

Originally set in the floor of a chapel, Nahl's monument commemorates the wife of the parish priest who died, with her child, on Easter Eve. The image of the grave slab being broken open soon became widely celebrated and was reproduced not only in engravings but also in replicas in wax and porcelain. Shortly after its completion the poet Christopher Martin Wieland described how the spirit of the sculptor had been able 'to command the dead stone to live and the souls to breathe in marble', and a writer in 1795 could claim that Nahl had represented 'with the whole power of victorious truth the decisive moment when Time and Eternity are joined, the transition from Death to Immortality'.

Monument to Princess Charlotte, (1796–1817) by Matthew Cotes Wyatt (1777–1862) Erected 1820–24. St George's Chapel, Windsor.

The Princess' death in childbirth was the occasion for public mourning that found expression in poetry, commemorative pottery and designs for her monument. After much public discussion a design was produced by a sculptor with experience in stage design. Above the powerful image of the shrouded corpse, surrounded by four draped figures representing the four corners of the world, rises the resurrected soul of the princess. The imagery of the Assumption of the Virgin is here adopted to Protestant use, making it an unambiguous expression of belief in eternal life.

never cease to wonder at the extreme folly of men, who erect such magnificent memorials to a handful of ashes and a few old bones.

Not surprisingly the process of bodily corruption and decay to which Bossuet refers appears on monuments only by implication or coded allusion, presented in emblematic, conventionalized forms such as the *memento mori* devices of skull and bones. But the physical reality of death was very familiar not only to those who contemplated such monuments but also to the sculptors who designed and executed them. Images of the deceased were sometimes even based on death masks bringing the sculptor into direct contact with the corpse, and occasionally this connection became grimly vivid. For example, in 1759 the sculptor Joseph Wilton, before designing his monument in Westminster Abbey to General Wolfe, went to Portsmouth to see the General's corpse as soon as it arrived from Canada; he was unable to take a death mask because its features had become too decayed.

In a few cases an awareness of the physical nature of death is expressed more directly in a three-dimensional form. A sculptural manifestation of this is seen in the anatomical models in wax produced around 1700 by Gaetano Giulio Zummo for a Parisian surgeon. Earlier Zummo had worked in Florence where the anatomist Francesco Redi was studying the decomposition of bodies. At this time the sculptor modelled his relief *The Corruption of the Body* (pl. 3a), in which a mourning allegorical figure of a conventional type is seated on a tomb containing, and surrounded by, rotting corpses. By placing the tomb within the context of decomposition and decay Zummo is stating what monuments left unsaid. Nonetheless, the society that produced grand and elaborate monuments, perpetuating the memory of earthly achievements, also encouraged the dissection of corpses and was indeed fascinated by the process of death. Anatomical models, tableaux of syphilitic corpses (pl. 3b) and marble monuments form part of a single visual culture, each representing a different way of making sense of death, life and the afterlife.

Unlike medieval monuments, in which an effigy of the

deceased is juxtaposed with a half decomposed body, eighteenth-century monuments usually introduce death not as a rotting corpse but personified in the form of a skeleton. While the earthly achievements of the Maréchal de Saxe are celebrated in the form of Hercules (representing his military strength) and the animals that symbolize the various European powers he vanquished, the main action consists of the confrontation between the heroic figure of Saxe and the figure of Death, which the female personification of France unsuccessfully attempts to ward off (pl. 4).

The horror of death is more dramatically presented in Schlüter's Männlich monument (pl. 5). Allegorical expressions of the qualities of the deceased are here abandoned in favour of a brutal image of the skeletal figure seizing a child, observed with horror by a figure whose role is not to personify a virtue but to register a horrific response to the scene.

Like Schlüter's Männlich monument, the Nightingale tomb by Roubiliac is for a married couple and expresses a private rather than a public grief (pl. 6). Although the work was originally commissioned by the couple's son, its design and execution between 1758 and 1761 were probably supervised by their recently widowed son-in-law, the husband of the daughter at whose birth the mother had died. The confrontation between Death, stepping out from the sarcophagus, and Lady Nightingale, vainly shielded by her husband, is therefore far more specific in its meaning than in the similar confrontation in Pigalle's Saxe monument. The menacing action of Death and the husband's protective response give the Nightingale monument its immediate dramatic force. Placed above the spectator's eye level, framed by what is almost a proscenium arch, the couple play out the action on the stage, the edge of which is clutched by Death's bony hand as he threatens to enter and destroy the shared life of man and wife above. But while an eighteenth-century public would, of course, have been gripped by the action as are modern observers, contemporary literature suggests that Death would not have been seen merely as a threat.

Works such as Edward Young's *Night Thoughts on Life, Death and Immortality* (1742) and many mid-eighteenth-century devotional writings presented death as a deliverer from earthly cares and a transportation to eternal life. Intended for a family closely connected with the Evangelical movement and early Methodism, the Nightingale monument presents the moment of transition from this world to the next as an assertion of faith in the afterlife. It is therefore not surprising that John Wesley praised this and the Hargrave monument (showing a body rising from the grave) as the most Christian tombs in the Abbey.

While the afterlife is shown only by implication in the Nightingale monument, it is referred to more directly in both the Morosini and the Mitrowicz monuments. In the former the bishop is shown in an attitude of prayer, looking expectantly towards an upper heavenly zone, represented by the angel holding the drapery above him. The eternal is expressed in the Mitrowicz monument not in terms of gesture or the emotional intensity of the participants but through complex symbolism and personification. The dead man is crowned by Divine Love, while his earthly honours and achievements are recorded by Fame on a pyramid – which is understood to endure until the end of time and is here shown crumbling when confronted with eternity (pl. 2). Thus, in the Mitrowicz monument, the afterlife is represented by allegory, and by allusion to a system of symbols and myths, and in the Morosini it is suggested as something that lies off-stage, beyond the scene. Other tombs refer to it in a more explicit way.

The monument to Maria Magdalena Langhans, who died on Easter Eve 1751 with the child to whom she was about to give birth, takes the form, not of a wall-monument with allegorical figures and an epitaph about her virtues, but of a grave slab which breaks open as the souls of mother and child rise heavenwards (pl. 7). Although the fact that these deaths took place on Easter Eve makes the imagery particularly appropriate in this case, it belongs to a large number of monuments showing souls being resurrected. Here any celebration of earthly achievements is confined to the inscribed epitaph, and the agony of death in childbirth is implied rather than stated. In the emphasis given to the overtly Christian theme of redemption and resurrection, the imagery of the Nahl monument, like that of Wyatt's monument to Princess Charlotte in St George's Chapel, Windsor, (pl. 8) is to be read as an assertion of faith – and more particularly a Protestant faith – in a period of increasing religious scepticism.

Yet while the Wyatt and Nahl monuments represent confident statements about the hope of eternity, each shows a specific event that appears to be happening in time. In both cases the turning point of the action is the transition between this world and the next. Its presentation demands the use of dramatic devices in which the eternal and the temporal are juxtaposed, for by such means the tension is heightened between the earthly and the other-worldly. In the monuments to Princess Charlotte and Maria Langhans the doctrine of resurrection allows the body rising from the grave to be used as this dramatic device.

In the Nightingale and Männlich monuments the two worlds are separated by the image of the door of death, while on the Saxe tomb they are divided into two horizontal zones, the figure of France vainly trying to deter Death from linking them. For all these monuments such dramatic devices translate into visual terms a process of transition involving the earthly, the eternal and death.

Placed in this context, the statue episode in the Don Juan myth may be seen to have had for the audience of Mozart's opera a particular intensity that depended on contemporary perceptions of tomb sculpture. When the figure of the Commendatore comes alive, da Ponte is not only employing a convention about animated statuary, he is also bringing into play a set of far more powerful responses associated with the imagery of monuments. On a tomb monument a single stage in the process of transition between the earthly and the other-worldly is isolated and translated into stone, although, as in any narrative painting or sculpture, episodes before and after are implied. In the statue scene of the opera the same process of transition from this world to the next is presented as a continuing narrative. Mozart's operatic version of the confrontation combines two powerful sets of conventions: that of a drama which shows the sequence of events on stage, and of tomb sculpture which for so long had been the static intermediary between the earthly and the eternal.

Notes to Odzooks! A Man of Stone

The following sources have been used for this essay: P.Ariès, *The Hour of our Death*, London, 1981; M. Baker and D. Bindman, 'Roubiliac's Nightingale Monument', *Burlington Magazine*, 130, 1988; J. Białostocki, 'The Door of Death', *Jahrbuch der Hamburger Kunstsammlungen*, 18, 1973; F. Bleibaum, *Johann August Nahl*, Baden bei Wien, 1933; F. Cagnetta, 'Gaetano Giulio Zummo', Kunsthistorischen Institut, Florens, *Kunst des Barock in Toscana. Halieinische Forschungen*, 3rd series, 9, 1976; J.R. Gaborit, *Jean Baptiste Pigalle*, Paris, 1985; C. Kleisch, 'Zur Todesikonographie bei Andreas Schlüter', *Staatliche Museen zu Berlin, forschungen und Berichte*, 13, 1971; A. Laing, 'Fischer von Erlach's Monument to Wenzel, Count Wratislaw von Mitrowicz', *Umeni*, 33, 1985; J. McManners, *Death and the Enlightenment*, Oxford, 1981; N. Penny, 'English Church Monuments to Women who died in Childbirth between 1780 and 1835', *Journal of the Warburg and Courtauld Institutes*, 38, 1974; G. Semenzato, *La scultura veneta del seicento e del settecento*, Venice, 1966.

The Father's Revenge

PETER GAY

Sigmund Freud, attempting to account for the enduring power of Sophocles' *Oedipus Rex*, sought that power in its theme. 'There must be a voice within us', he wrote, 'which is ready to acknowledge the compelling force of fate in *Oedipus*.' Its protagonist's 'fate stirs us only because it could have been our own.' Freud had a rather utilitarian view of culture; he most enjoyed those poets, wits and dramatists who could enlarge his grasp on the human mind at work. While he did not insist that aesthetic pleasure is simply the dividend attached to instruction or entertainment, his whole mind was rarely on the performance. In 1912 he reported to Ferenczi that he had just come from a performance of *Don Giovanni*. In the second act, during the festive supper that the Don has ordered, the hired band plays a snatch from Mozart's *Marriage of Figaro*, and Leporello comments: 'that music seems very familiar to me.' Freud found 'a good application to the current situation' – his deteriorating relationship with Jung. The music he was hearing now was music he had heard before in 1906, when his long and passionate friendship with Fliess had ended on a sour note. Even *Don Giovanni*, his favourite opera, did not wholly drive business out of his mind. But what particularly concerned him with *Oedipus Rex* as a psychoanalyst was its special, far from obvious resonance. He found in it the nuclear complex, the fate that Oedipus shares with us all. Does the same dynamic animate *Don Giovanni*? In this essay I want to follow in Freud's footsteps and explore the opera's hidden agenda, the compelling force that awakens the voice within us to response.

While Oedipal pressures certainly animated Wolfgang Amadeus Mozart, I do not intend to read a complex work of art, one standing in a rich literary and operatic tradition, as the simple translation of its maker's repressed unconscious childhood traumas. The chemistry of creation remains to be analysed and synthesized. It is impermissible to reduce art to a substitute activity – a mere response to (or triumph over) neurosis. But we do find in art reparation for childish crimes – largely imaginary but no less troubling for that. We also find the sublimation of erotic and hostile wishes.

Each province of the mind, the id, the ego, the superego, must somehow be satisfied in the act of creation which celebrates a truce in the maker's mental economy, a liberation of energies. Moreover, each work of art is a work of memory, a representation of things seen, heard, felt and stored away. Nor do these elements alone make the landscape, the sonnet – or the opera. They must be fostered by the pleasure in mastery, by that aggression to which Freud sometimes assigned the stature of a separate drive. The psychological balance making for creativity in one artist will differ from that governing another. If, in Munch or Mahler, we sense the shaping force of neurotic pressures – art as confession – we find few such intimations in Rubens or Mozart. Ego strength is an element in the making of art as much as is ego weakness, and all this is, of course, not enough: the vast, elaborate machinery of craftsmanship, rationally acquired and exercised, has its share in the making of art.

All this said, I do, nevertheless, want to suggest that the dominant theme of *Don Giovanni* replays Mozart's own real-life battles. Of course, the suggestion must remain tentative: for all of Mozart's outpouring of letters, for all his colourful and uninhibited speech, he held back much of himself. Moreover, as Wolfgang Hildesheimer has rightly insisted, Mozart had a marked capacity for separating his feelings from his work. Yet there is something poignant and profoundly personal about the timing of *Don Giovanni*. It is one of those accidents that was no accident.

Leopold Mozart died at the end of May 1787. Aware of his

father's illness, Wolfgang Mozart was working on *Don Giovanni*. The impulse for a new opera had been the success of *The Marriage of Figaro*, which had induced an impresario in Prague to offer Mozart a contract for a new opera. Early in 1787, moreover, Gazzaniga's one-act comic opera, *Don Giovanni Tenorio*, had been performed in Venice, and served da Ponte as a welcome stimulant. But it was Mozart's exquisitely ambivalent feelings about his father that gave his music for da Ponte's libretto a particular seriousness and psychological penetration. In his hands, *Don Giovanni* became a grand war between the generations in which the loser displays courage and dignity.

Leopold Mozart was not just a father to his genius son. He was gadfly, trainer, manager, adviser, impresario; as a composer of modest distinction but professional standing, he was, in addition, an expert to be respected, an ego ideal to be lived up to – and a towering figure to be fought. He mercilessly drove the infant prodigy that nature had dropped into his lap, though there is evidence that little Wolfgang, with his wig and his toy sword, enjoyed his celebrity. Eminent personages spoiled him, and the exhausting tours he took with his father satisfied his alert sense of curiosity and need for adventure. Yet, almost from the beginning, there was a necessary strain between father and son, the more ineradicable, no doubt, for being largely unconscious. Wolfgang Amadeus Mozart was Leopold Mozart's obedient son, whose hands he kissed (at least in subscribing his letters) a thousand times, whose counsel he sought and whose good opinion he continued to crave into adulthood.

Nevertheless, fairly early it must have become obvious to both that the son was the father's superior. The quality of the son's compositions surpassed his father's rather lame efforts with sovereign ease. The son's facility in composing, too, was strikingly beyond the reach of his father's laboured ways. Wolfgang Amadeus Mozart could imagine one piece of music while copying down another, and 'see' a complete composition in his head before he had put a note on paper. There is a much-quoted sentence from a letter to his father which has sometimes been written off as boasting within the family, but which seems to describe, quite soberly, the intensity of Mozart's absorption in his world: 'Komponirt ist schon alles – aber geschrieben noch nicht' ('Everything is already composed, but not yet written down').

That letter dates from the end of December, 1780. Around this time the son was beginning to test his independence in those domains that mattered most to him: his erotic life and his self-esteem. In both tests, he aroused his father's worry, and anger. But he persisted. In 1781, his crisis year, the younger Mozart was twenty-five. He found, not to his surprise, that his father approved neither of his future wife, Constanze Weber, nor of his decision to leave the service of his employer, the insensitive Archbishop of Salzburg. As he told his father in dignified, almost pathetic pleas, he must save his honour – but he only received new reproaches.

Mozart recognized the rift that had opened between him and his father, a rift that politeness could paper over but time could not heal. He did not cease professing his obedience, but the formula served mainly to contain his disappointment at his father's lack of empathy for his libidinal needs and for his self-respect. And beneath his conscious rage, there boiled an unconscious rage against his father, disciplinarian and exploiter, who was trying to keep him subservient to paternal authority years after he had reached his maturity. As a little boy, he had liked to say, 'Next after God comes my father'. But then, he had never been very religious.

Many of Mozart's operas are organized around the struggle between generations. *Idomeneo*, Mozart's finest *opera seria*, is at bottom about a father's cannibalistic wishes against his son, peacefully resolved. In contrast, *Die Entführung aus dem Serail* is an amusing entertainment in which the young lovers are given their freedom, and thus the opportunity to marry, by a humane – and somewhat elderly – pasha, who really wants the girl, Constanze, for himself, but chooses not to exercise his power.

A very similar motif, with a paternal figure not so self-denying, informs *Le nozze di Figaro*. The Count thinks of reintroducing the feudal *ius primae noctis* just for the sake of enjoying the charming Susanna. But she is engaged, and faithful, to Figaro. The denouement is not unexpected: the Count is compelled to yield to the young couple. But what matters, and had been foreshadowed in the Beaumarchais play that served da Ponte for a model, is that the Count finds himself obliged to ask everyone's forgiveness. Conflict issues in reconciliation, the victory of the young brings not revenge but a feast. *The Magic Flute*, too, fits into this pattern. Once again the younger generation, strengthened in trust by the trials imposed by the older generation, emerges triumphant. Mozart's late *opera seria*, *La Clemenza di Tito*, has a rather different, involuted intrigue, but its conclusion is also one of harmony restored and made possible by the forgiveness of the all-powerful.

These have been conventional plots for centuries; dozens of librettists in Mozart's time, and before, had exploited them to the full. Their popularity says something about their cultural resonance and about the unconscious need for forgiveness to be dramatized. But their popularity with Mozart testifies to his own buried needs. His ambivalence toward his father was exacerbated by his guilt-ridden conviction that he had already bested him, and that he was confirming his easy superiority with each new composition. And his remorse must have become particularly acute during the spring and summer of 1787, when he was doing his work of mourning for a father he had intensely loved and hated. His sense of supremacy must have been poisoned, not by the anguish of guilt alone, but by the fear of revenge. And this, in significant measure, is what *Don Giovanni* is about.

True, the three main protagonists around whom da Ponte devised the plot are not those of the conventional Oedipal triangle intrinsic to the contest between father and son. Donna Anna, after all, is not the Don's mother. Nor is she the Commendatore's wife. But we know that the mind, leaving its deposits in works of the imagination, is awash with defensive manœuvres, with efforts to clean up shocking situations – efforts that often fail. Nothing would be easier for the unconscious than to transform a mother into a young and desirable woman, especially since, when the little boy desired his mother, she was both young and desirable.

Further evidence for an Oedipal reading of *Don Giovanni* is strewed across the opera. Donna Anna is taboo for Don Giovanni not just because she is a virginal, aristocratic young lady, but because she is bound to another man. Moreover, her response to her father's death has a fierce emotionality pervaded by an air of hysterical overemphasis and compulsive repetition which reveals a very special sort of mourning. When Don Ottavio offers to marry Donna Anna, she tells him, almost in so many words, that she can think only of her father. Again, in the concluding sextet, she asks Don Ottavio – it has often been noted – to postpone their marriage for a year. Her pathetic plea has been read, particularly by commentators following E. T. A. Hoffmann, as a kind of slip, revealing her secret infatuation with Don Giovanni.

In Hoffmann's famous novella, 'Don Juan', the Don, just before the curtain rises on the opera, has consummated his conquest of Donna Anna in the obscurity of her maidenly bedroom and aroused in her a criminal love for her irresistible seducer. This is possible; certainly Mozart scholars like Alfred Einstein have made Hoffmann's version their own. But it is quite as likely, and indeed psychologically more persuasive, to think of Donna Anna as continuing to mourn, not for the Don, but for her father. Hers is an attachment whose implications she doubtless fails to understand, an attachment with horrendous incestuous overtones. Her unabating excitement, her calls for vengeance punctuated by moments of sad passivity and near collapse, suggest nothing less. It is significant that Don Ottavio calls himself Anna's 'husband and father'.

In the opera, we do not know, we shall never know, what happened in Donna Anna's bedroom. Hoffmann's narrator sees the face of Donna Anna upon her first appearance marked by 'love, rage, hatred, despair'. To Hoffmann, this palette of contradictory emotions permits only one explanation: the loss of her virginity to the Don, at once humiliating, terrifying, and secretly enjoyed. Whether we are watching the aftermath of rape or the unfolding of a fantasy, Donna Anna must regard any erotic commerce with Don Giovanni as a betrayal of her father quite as much as a gross insult to her spirit and her body. Whatever happened in that bedroom, Don Giovanni's duel with the Commendatore seems remarkably like a symbolic patricide.

Such a reading is particularly persuasive in view of the way Mozart and da Ponte interpret the character of Don Giovanni. Unable to stay with an erotic object, reinvesting his libido almost daily like a feverish speculator on the stock exchange of love, Don Giovanni seems to have but a single purpose: to appease a nagging hunger, a hunger which no satisfaction can relieve more than momentarily. He seems to be trying to prove something about his potency, his manliness, always in doubt.

Conventional psychoanalytic wisdom sees Don Juan in an aura of homosexual panic. Yet this diagnosis finds limited support in the opera. Don Giovanni's exuberance sounds unforced; his bravery, though extraordinary, is too secure, too relaxed, to be a mere cloak for repressed doubts. There is only one hint of perversity: his greatest passion – Leporello tells Donna Elvira in the catalogue aria – is the young beginner, the barely nubile girl who, at her time of life, is just emerging from latency. But this is surely not enough on which to hang a diagnosis of latent homosexuality.

Rather, his restless inability to find lasting gratification with anyone, of any rank, any shape, any character, suggests an unresolved Oedipal fixation. Don Giovanni, ever unsatisfied and ever dissatisfied, finally seeks to consummate an early yearning for conquest, dearly wished and never achieved, and never to be made good no matter how long Leporello's list may in the end become. The Don knows in his heart that each new conquest must fail him, yet he is compelled to try again. What lies concealed in the Don's aggressive energy is, in addition to his libidinal drive, his rage against a world that once denied him what he most craved. This is why he shows no remorse at having murdered the Commendatore. Conscious of his youth and suppleness as a duellist, he warned him, but when Donna Anna's father persists, the Don coolly finishes him off.

The Don finishes off the Commendatore and does not finish him off. He finds that there is no way of exorcizing the father. He has killed the old man in a struggle over a woman, yet, as by a miracle, the old man lives on. The psychoanalyst, alert to such tricks of the mind, is not likely to be puzzled by such supernatural events. The dead father lives on to take his revenge – in his victim's mind. What is more the ghostly internalized authority figure, like a typical tyrannical father – or a typical punitive superego – not merely orders the son to hell, but wants him to feel remorse in the process. The father wants repentance and a show of submission. But the son refuses, over and over, and thus turns this episode, which Mozart's predecessors had treated as rather routine, into one of the most thrilling moments in the history of the theatre.

The Don is perhaps posturing a little, as though his manliness were, if not at stake, at least in play: he exclaims that no one will ever accuse him of cowardice. But, considering his extreme situation, he does more than merely talk heroism. He embodies it. Even after the Statue has taken his hand and chilled him to the marrow, he persists in setting the defiance of the young against the authority of the old. *Repent, change your life*, the Statue commands, *change – this is your last chance*. But though the Don cannot free himself from the Statue's icy grip, he only asks it to be gone. The Commendatore, voice of conscience, tries again: *Repent, wretch*. But the Don matches his executioner insult for insult: *No! old fool!*

The argument continues:

Repent!
No!
Repent!
No!

with finally, a desperate attempt at persuasion in which Leporello joins,

Yes!

But Don Giovanni, heroic to the end, explodes his last great refusal:

No!

In vain. The world of the father, the world of unquestioned authority, is still in control. Nevertheless, though the Don is doomed, our overwhelming reaction springs from the power of his challenge to that authority. The world of the son, we feel, is still to come. In his description of the Oedipus complex Freud called attention to the different ways that Sophocles and Shakespeare dramatize the theme. Their markedly divergent treatment suggested to Freud that cultural styles change across the centuries. By the time of *Don Giovanni*, repression had gone, but another psychological process, the rise of the younger generation, had entered the arena.

The mocker of Seville is of course, an old story. One can trace it to folk tales, witness it in primitive performances at fairs, and read it from the early seventeenth century on. The Don scorns God and man alike, and his contempt for conventional mores only underscores his cold indifference to the divine order. His fickle love of women, wholesale, irresponsible, cruel, greedy, is just another form of blasphemy. It offers violence to all that is sacred.

Mozart and da Ponte lent this story a new energy and a new point. That energy – which is part of the point – surfaces in some surprising places. Consider the Don's shortest aria in the first act. This spirited tirade is a set of instructions to Leporello on just how to entertain Zerlina, Masetto and their companions until the Don can have his way with Zerlina. It speaks forcibly for the vitality that the wicked son radiates, the pleasure he gives even his victims.

From the founding of the tradition, Don Juan Tenorio had been something better than a vulgar seducer. Mozart and da Ponte make him, with all his vices, all his low appetites, into a rebel of the highest order. Students of Mozart have not failed to observe that he wrote his operas around the years of the French Revolution; especially in *Le nozze di Figaro* they have professed to find hints at political rebelliousness against a social order founded on birth rather than regulated by merit. Mozart was certainly not a political thinker, and neither wrote nor implied political manifestos. What does appear plainly in his work, and in his correspondence, is something more sweeping: the all-human theme of human authority, an authority threatened, at times overthrown, at times saved by compromise.

For centuries, political institutions, like the religious beliefs their rulers shared and manipulated, have been constructed on the pattern of the family. The monarch, like the high priest, like God, or the gods, is a father of his country. This is more than a metaphor: to establish a dynasty is a way of perpetuating the rule of one family against the claims of rivals. But the laws of succession are not simply a self-serving device. They are designs for stability. 'The King is dead, long live the King!' is a proclamation that bears heavy emotional freight. The death of the ruler is a rent in the social fabric. But in the unconscious – and often enough in conscious life through the persistence of tradition – the dead past continues to govern its future.

Modern theories of social contract and of constitutionalism, first developed in the late sixteenth century, and finding their classic expression a century later with Lockian liberalism, were designed to diffuse institutionalized paternal authority. But at home, the father's legal, moral, and psychological authority remained unimpaired. And the patriarchal theory of government continued to have its advocates. In the days of the Glorious Revolution, John Locke found it necessary to refute in painful detail Sir Rober Filmer's view of governance that saw the state as the family writ large, and the father's rights over his wife and children as models for the king's rights over his subjects. Yet, while many thought this seventeenth-century theory antiquated, even absurd, powerful Continental states – Russia, Prussia, France – continued on their absolutist course. It was this that the French Revolution attacked and in part, demolished.

But history, like the mind, has its hidden continuities. The Revolution in France was as great a break in the historical process as it is possible to imagine. It reached, in public law and private habit, down into the most fundamental relations human beings know, those laying down the respective obligations of parents and children. The Don's last *No!* was the manifesto of a son ready to take up arms against his father. And yet the Statue's ultimate triumph was a sign that the campaign was not yet – nor, perhaps, would ever be – won.

From this perspective the much debated concluding sextet in Mozart's opera may reclaim its place as the natural conclusion of the work. It is bound to fall a little flat after the excitement of the unsurpassable scene that preceded it. Like all restorations it is inevitably less fascinating than the revolutions it follows and seeks to undo. But it is a logically – for Mozart and da Ponte at least, a *psychologically* – necessary scene. It marks the re-emergence of order after chaos, shows the ordinary laws of life regaining their authority after their near overthrow. It is the calm after the storm, a sly reminder that in the great Oedipal war it is perhaps safer to lose than to win.

The Libertine's Progress

PETER CONRAD

The archetypal character wants to go everywhere, and to become everyone. He is less a person than a potential, whose migration through time, place and metamorphic changes of identity declare his ambition to experience an infinitude of possibilities. Europe has three such tireless, recurrent seekers in its mythology – Faust, the man of mind who wants to know everything; Robinson Crusoe, the economic man who wants to own everything; and Don Juan, the man of the senses who intends both to know and to own everything, and whose mode of doing so is to make love. Since their ambitions are global, the careers of these characters last for centuries. In the course of their intercontinental, even extraterrestrial journeying, they alter and contradict themselves at will: the mythic creature survives in history by mutating; eternity puts on camouflage for its descent into time.

Thus the Faust who is in medieval versions a spiritual criminal has become, for Goethe, a justified romantic rebel, condemned only when he pauses in his quest; while the Crusoe who is, for Defoe, a monopolistic bourgeois from the first heroic phase of capitalism, can turn into a haunted solipsist as Coleridge's ancient mariner, or an alienated modern self as Conrad's Martin Decoud. The same versatility is the inexhaustible resource of Don Juan. The seventeenth-century blasphemer, mocking God in the play by Tirso de Molina, changes to an eighteenth-century epicurean, who asks no more than his right to life, liberty and the pursuit of happiness, then to a nineteenth-century idealist and, after that, in the twentieth century, declines into a suitable case for psychiatric treatment. Freud's colleague Otto Rank, having seen *Don Giovanni* in Vienna in 1921, wrote a diagnosis of the legend assessing the libertine not as a man but a 'psychic mechanism', an anthropomorphized complex. His problem, Rank surmised, was Oedipal: his crime was the fancied killing of a father. And the multifarious women he loved and left were substitutes for the unobtainable mother he so guiltily desired.

In every period, he is quick to establish himself as a contemporary by learning new tricks and trades. The man who is synonymous with philandering can even risk dissociating himself from sex. To Shaw, he's an abstinent socialist; for Max Frisch, another of his recreators, a modern Juan ought to exchange sensual connoisseurship for scientific knowledge, physicality for physics. Since Juan's obsession is to understand the workings of nature, Frisch advises him to advance from the bedroom to the laboratory, and go to work on splitting the atom.

The first sponsor of this prolific offspring, in the play atributed to Tirso de Molina and dating probably from 1616, is located in ethical orthodoxy. *El Burlador de Sevilla* is monkish propaganda, demonstrating the vengeful triumph of death. The 'burlador' burlesques religion, and is punished by the heaven he offends. By 1664, when Molière wrote his *Dom Juan*, the cultural judgment of the character has shifted. The jesting apostate is now a philosopher. Whereas the Juans of the eighteenth century – most obviously Don Giovanni – live for pleasure, Molière's hero is driven by a rational curiosity, prising open the fissure between moral pretence and carnal truth. He enjoys the disguise of Sganarelle (his Leporello) as a physician, for he too is ministering to the body by elucidating its appetites.

Sizing up a likely conquest, Molière's Juan studies assets as clinically as if he were undertaking a medical check-up. He demands to know the condition of Charlotte's teeth. Sganarelle calls him an unbeliever, but his atheism is a dictate of intellectual logic, neither a superstitious insanity (as for Tirso) nor a sublime satanism (as for E.T.A. Hoffmann or Baudelaire). He laughs at the marble mausoleum and the statue of the Commander for a good reason: he's appalled by the conceit of a corpse which wants a custom-built palace to moulder in. Mozart's Giovanni in the graveyard derides the notion of an afterlife. Molière's Juan bothers rather about biological justice in this present life. Thus his quarrel with the patriarchal Commander is extended to his own father. Wishing the old man would stop lecturing him and lie down to die, Juan promulgates a law of nature, criticizing the indiscretion of fathers who outlive their sons, just as – when he offers to give a beggar alms if the fellow will blaspheme – he is endeavouring to tutor him in self-reliance, not corrupting him.

If Moliere's Tartuffe is hypocritical about the sacred, his Juan is honest about the profane. He means it when he tells Elvira that he's sincere, and has no skill at pretending. It's this disinterested truth-telling which makes him so cruel and so dangerous. For other Don Juans, the catalogue is a smirking black book of telephone numbers. For Molière's man, it's a calculus, testifying to his faith in the incorruptibility of arithmetic, and to his encyclopaedic meticulousness – he is scrupulously fair, he explains to Sganarelle, so he can't deny any woman her right to his attention just because he happens to be married to another. When Sganarelle demands to know what he believes in (since he refuses to credit God, ghosts or the devil), Juan replies that he believes two and two are four, and four and four are eight. Leporello, unreeling Don Giovanni's list, pauses at a figure which stands for incompleteness, the indefinite postponement of an end: 'mille e tre'. His thousand and three successes in Spain, like Scheherazade's thousand and one tales, are randomly excerpted from a total which will be innumerable. Molière's Juan juggles with more concrete sums, and makes equations from them. Promiscuity is an exercise in learning the multiplication table.

Mozart's Don Giovanni compounds this version of the character with a different evaluation which soon replaces it, adding to the classic reason of Molière's sexual mathematician a tempestuous romantic irrationality. At the end of the eighteenth century, Don Giovanni inaugurates the nineteenth. Confined to the earlier period, he is a hedonist who derives his manners from Rousseau, or from Sterne's susceptible Yorick in *A Sentimental Journey*. Zeffirelli's production at Covent Garden placed him in a

Watteauesque pleasure garden; Losey's film billeted him in a Palladian villa near Vicenza. But Don Giovanni strains forward into the later period, casting off the role of seducer and revealing as his deeper motive a demonic challenge to God. Hence Peter Hall's updating of him at Glyndebourne to a sallow Regency rake, menaced by retributive thunderstorms, who had given up delectation for metaphysical combat.

The operatic hero owes his complexity to the ambiguous partnership of words and music. In da Ponte's text, Don Giovanni remains the unsparing cynic of the eighteenth century, like Don Alfonso in *Così fan tutte* or that anatomist of pleasure's divine imperatives, the 'Marquis' de Sade. But from that first announcement of death in the overture, and the scurrying vital volatility which it excites into being, Mozart's music grants to da Ponte's Casanova an intensity and desperation which launch him on his exploration of the nineteenth century.

Don Giovanni's existence is musical not verbal, and his music, as Kierkegaard argued, has such sensuous immediacy that we seem to be listening to the life-force, fleetly keeping ahead of mortality and exuberantly protesting against extinction. Eduard Mörike, in the story he wrote in 1855 about Mozart's journey to Prague for the first production of *Don Giovanni*, has the composer describe the final scene as his own disappearance into the sublime vastness of landscape, elated by the destruction which merges him with what Wordsworth called 'the one life within us and abroad'. Instead of descending to the inferno, Don Giovanni is pantheistically absorbed into nature. 'Now, of course, there was no stopping me', says Mörike's Mozart; he feels himself fall through cracking ice into the depths of a lake, and when the devils seize Don Giovanni he likens his own 'horror and fascination' – constituents of the romantic sublime – to 'our sensations when nature unleashes its force in an avalanche or a great fire: in spite of ourselves we . . . side with that blind power'. This romantic agony is also a fierce ecstasy.

Redeemed by his sacrifice, the nineteenth century's Don Juan began to resemble the altruistic Faust. Nikolaus Lenau's version of him in 1851 is no skirt-chaser but a yearning dreamer, intent on

the idea of 'a woman who is the incarnation of womanhood' –
Goethe's 'ewig Weibliche' who leads us upwards. To suit this
revisionism, new music had to be written for the libertine.
Richard Strauss's symphonic poem *Don Juan* (1889), taking its
plot from Lenau, abandons the repressive morality with which
Tirso and his successors had persecuted Juan, and which Mahler
censored when he cut Mozart's smug final sextet from his
performances of *Don Giovanni*. No stone guest chills the flesh of
Strauss's character; the tragedy now is the lyrically lively body's
debilitation by age, and Strauss narrates the elderly hero's revival
in memory of his youthful ardour. Words here renounce all claim
on Don Juan. Because he is, to the romantics, the incarnation of
music, at odds with the fretful consciousness of language, Strauss
returns him to speechlessness. He *is* the orchestra; the tone poem
distils the opera.

Romanticism subversively adopted and rewrote *Don Giovanni*
as a sacrilegious scripture. Hoffmann – who saw himself as
Mozart's imaginative progeny, and legitimized the descent by
assuming Amadeus as one of his middle names – acclimatized the
work to his own heretical creed in his fable 'Don Juan', published
in 1813. In 1843, Kierkegaard used the opera to elaborate the
dialectic of his treatise *Either/Or*, in which he opposes the dull
wisdom of ethics to the happy irresponsibility of aesthetics.

Kierkegaard's aesthete, a prophet of romanticism, takes the
operas of Mozart as an infidel holy writ and an amoral conduct-
book. 'Never before', he proposes, 'has sensuousness been
conceived as it is in *Don Giovanni* – as a principle'; and that
conception originates necessarily in opera, because 'the genius of
sensuousness is . . . the absolute subject of music', tuning up the
receptive human body and overhearing the song which streams
from it.

The eroticism which Kierkegaard's dialectician expounds
evolves through three stages, and each is personified by Mozart.
First is the indiscriminate daydreaming of the page in *Le Nozze di
Figaro*, harmlessly neutered, for Cherubino is a Don Giovanni
with undescended testicles. Next comes the wedded fertility of
Papageno in *Die Zauberflöte*, so anxious for a mate and a brood of

children. Kierkegaard deplores *Die Zauberflöte* because it allows the music of the senses to be 'ethically determined', positing married love as its aim; and, as a 'Singspiel', it has made the libertine spirit of music accountable once more to pettifogging, prohibitive words. Bypassing this, the third and highest stage is represented by Don Giovanni, in whom desire incites an intoxicated tumult. His hunting ground is not the Seville of Tirso but a place known to the anatomical cartography of the Middle Ages: that occult paradise called the mound of Venus, or the Venusberg – 'there the sensuous has its home', says Kierkegaard, 'there it has its own wild pleasures, for it is a kingdom, a state'; and there Wagner, a generation later, will imprison his own decadent, sated Don Giovanni – the character who goes by the name of Tannhäuser.

As the libertine proceeds through these permutations of identity, his victims undergo corresponding changes. Kierkegaard's theory depends on a reinterpretation of Elvira. She is defined as Don Giovanni's 'mortal enemy', or 'his epic fate, as the Commendatore is his dramatic fate'. Having been seduced, she has been hurt into self-awareness, and this knowledge makes her deadly to Don Giovanni, who can never pause long enough to discover anything about himself. But despite her hatred, she can't kill him. Molière's Elvira warns Don Juan to repent because she has passed beyond vindictiveness to a detached concern for his welfare – a lucid condition like his own attitude to the pious beggar. Kierkegaard's Elvira has no such rational purpose; she rails at Don Giovanni but she still loves him, and therefore must both curse and pardon him. Kierkegaard calls her an epic antagonist because, if the action were left to her and Don Giovanni, the opera would go on forever, like a clash between Titans leading always to stalemate. Only the Commendatore can dramatically terminate the work. Elvira transmits her mixed motives to later analyses of the raging eternal woman. Otto Rank argues that Don Giovanni's view of the vampirish female is confirmed by Wagner's Isolde, who (like Elvira) vows to slay Tristan yet when the sword is offered to her lets it drop.

While Kierkegaard's investigation names Elvira as the clue to

Don Giovanni's deepest fears, Hoffmann concentrates on Donna Anna who, seditiously reinterpreted, is Don Giovanni's spiritual bride. Hoffmann's way with Mozart's opera is the devil's who quotes scripture to serve his private purpose, for Satan is the promoter of romantic literary criticism, expert at enticing unlawful meanings from texts. Hoffmann begins by attributing his visionary experience of the opera to this agent, who is Don Giovanni's ally: he hears the overture in his sleep and asks, 'Could it be that Satan, who is never idle when it comes to mischief, had bewitched me?' Lured by the sound, he goes to hear *Don Giovanni* in a provincial theatre, and is phantasmagorically joined in his box by the singer of Donna Anna. She uses the cubicle as a confessional, admitting to Hoffmann that her revulsion against Giovanni has turned, after his death, into infatuation. Their mystic marriage can be consummated only if she chooses to share his perdition. The feverish soprano dies that same night, at the precise moment when Hoffmann hears, again in his sleep, an aerial orchestra playing Donna Anna's aria 'Non mi dir'. For Kierkegaard, Elvira symbolizes the sensuous urgency of music. For Hoffmann, Donna Anna is that muse: acknowledging that he too is a composer, she says she has sung in his operas – 'I am your melodies'.

The Don Giovanni in Hoffmann's performance has 'a Mephistophelean look', and the infernal nay-sayer, the critical spirit of contradiction, lends his techniques to the narrative. Hoffmann's story is a model of the inquisitorial method whereby romanticism extorts forbidden significance from classic works. Hoffmann's concern is the 'inner meaning' of *Don Giovanni*. That meaning, retrieved, cancels the opera's warranty (flaunted in its subtitle) to punish dissoluteness: Don Giovanni is acclaimed by Hoffmann as a rival of God, not a mere menace to women. He outrages a divine creation; Hoffmann imitates him by ingeniously disfiguring Mozart's creation. His libertine-like tactic for liberating the truth is a seductive ingratiation – a sideways entry. He gets into the opera house from his inn through a concealed door, which opens onto a short passage and then onto Loge 23. What he sees on stage is a flagrant Donna Anna whose clinging nightgown, as she grapples with Don Giovanni, 'suggests and scarcely conceals provocative charms': her physique stands for the forbidden body of the work, exposed by Hoffmann's analysis.

Having uncovered *Don Giovanni*'s secret, Hoffmann protects his testimony by obscuring it all over again. Just as, in opera, words can only approximate to the potent inarticulate eloquence of music, so Hoffmann must impotently translate across a gap between musical desire and verbal understanding. He converses with Donna Anna in her native Tuscan, then recounts her confidences in a letter to his friend Theodore: 'but when I try to write down in German what she said, every word appears stiff and dull to me, every phrase clumsy, incapable of expressing what, in Tuscan, she put so easily and gracefully'. Music, like poetry, gets lost in the translation. Hoffmann's writing, or the reported speech with which the story ends (as the guests at the inn curtly tell him of the singer's death), are the verbal leftovers of a truth expressible only by music.

In England, however – defying the injunctions against language of both Hoffmann and Kierkegaard – the libertine appears as a garrulous talker. The hero of Byron's *Don Juan* is more an anecdotalist than a seducer, and the vastly chatty poem through which he wanders transforms libertinism into a parliamentary liberalism. It is, as G. K. Chesterton said of Browning's *The Ring and the Book*, 'an epic of free speech'. Thus it is, potentially, interminable. No 'dramatic fate' like Kierkegaard's curtails it and, when the stone guest arrives, it is as one more conquest for Giovanni. He touches the spectre into palpability, and lays bare the Duchess of Fitz-Fulke; there the poem, which knows it can't end, simply breaks off.

In what Shaw called his 'Don Juan play', *Man and Superman* (1905), the radical Tanner proselytizes in preference to making love. Leporello's catalogue is rewritten as a manual for distribution to revolutionaries. When, in Shaw's hell, his characters metamorphose into Mozart's, the hectic velocity of Don Giovanni's champagne aria is replaced by a marathon of palaver. 'Go on talking', is the patronizing dismissal by Ann (Shaw's Donna Anna) of her logorrheal consort. This, of course, lames Don

Giovanni, who is now the abject prey of an Ibsenite new woman. Leporello, meanwhile, has been educated, and put through an engineering course at a polytechnic to qualify as Tanner's driver. The musical demons have been verbally mechanized.

When Don Giovanni returns to opera, he is the relic of his romantic self. Tom Rakewell, in the text written by Auden and Chester Kallman for Stravinsky's *The Rake's Progress* (1951), digests an anthology of erstwhile Don Giovannis. Though he begins in Hogarth's satiric etchings, he graduates to the nineteenth century. Propounding his carefree gospel in the brothel, he is Byron's Don Juan, exonerated from any moral cares. But his travel through time brings him at last to the existential absurdity of the twentieth century, which calls the bluff of his liberty. Rakewell is no Hoffmannesque taunter of God; he's an atom in a materialistic universe, where fates depend on luck (as Sellem says in auctioning his effects) or games of chance (when Nick Shadow cuts the cards). The career of romanticism – which for Auden and Stravinsky is indistinguishable from the digressive vagaries of the libertine – ends, along with Rakewell, in the lunatic asylum.

A romantic optimism discouraged by European history takes refuge, however, in America, where there are constitutional amendments to protect the libertine's policy of moral *laissez-faire*. America was the destination of Mozart's librettist da Ponte, who died in New York; Eric Linklater sent Don Giovanni there in a novel called *Juan in America*, published in 1931. The Juan in question is a genealogical sprig of Byron's poem, germinated at that encounter with the Duchess of Fitz-Fulke. Linklater extends the libertine's life by gainsaying his meaning for, as Kierkegaard's condescension about Papageno's mating implies, it's impossible to imagine Don Giovanni with children. Indeed, in one of his posthumous American existences, he hands on his technique of promiscuous enumeration to homosexuals: the hustler in John Rechy's 1967 novel *Numbers* computes adventures at a rate which would have exhausted even Leporello, totting up thirty-seven 'lewd acts' during a single day in the public parks and back alleys of Los Angeles.

Summarizing the interim between Byron and the 1930s,

Linklater makes Juan a godchild of romantic philosophy. He owes his existence to the moral laxity disseminated by Tom Paine and William Godwin, who mock the sacrament of marriage. The very name of Linklater's character predestines him for a picaresque future: he is called Motley. This hero, who is himself a potentiality, belongs in America which is as Linklater says 'the land of infinite possibility'. Once he's there, he finds that his old satanic, dissipated style of life has been humanely and profitably revised. Leporello's catalogue, across the Atlantic, is a technological tool. Juan attends college to study Accountancy Principles and Commercial Statistics. During the nineteenth century, the libertine fuses with that other insubordinate archetype, Faust; in the twentieth century, which belongs to American capitalism, he merges with Crusoe. The numerosity of the new world has better things to do than tally sexual scores. It's more impressed by the sanitary fitments of the Hotel Connecticut, where Juan stays in Manhattan: 'Two thousand nine hundred and eighty rooms, two thousand nine hundred and eighty baths – this was its professional boast and official capacity'. As for women, the melting pot simplifies Juan's task by aggregating them all, and moulding the Statue of Liberty's 'huddled masses' into a single synthetic being. New York is a compilation of all the European cultures through which Don Giovanni roved, amalgamating 'the incurable adolescence of Ireland, the sentimental heart of Germany, and the lively passion of Italy'. Don Giovanni need no longer tiringly take census of all the categories Leporello mentions – 'la bionda', 'la bruna', 'la bianca' – because American democracy, singing what one of Linklater's characters calls its 'song of miscegenation', has intermarried them: 'Black shall mate with white, negro with northener, and the strength of Africa run hot in Nordic veins'.

The end comes for the emigrant libertine when America obliges him to reform, conform and pledge allegiance to the flag. This happens in 1949, in a Warner Brothers film called *Adventures of Don Juan*, directed by Vincent Sherman. The music is by Max Steiner not Mozart, and Don Juan is played by that alcoholic reprobate Errol Flynn, whose wicked, wicked ways the film might be expected to relate – but the truth is stranger.

Linklater had presented Juan's birth as an allegory of Whiggish progress. 'The eighteenth century was dying, and Time was already busy with a nursery for the nineteenth.' The lordly bastard is 'the coming child of Chronos'. Hollywood's Don Juan had the same chronological mission, serving what the noisy newsreels of the day called 'the march of time' or even, in Comte's terms, the march of mind. As the film begins, a montage of technical inventions is accompanied by a narrator with the avuncular authority of a commentator on *The March of Time*. His voice declares that 'At the beginning of the seventeenth century, mankind was climbing hand over hand, onwards, ever upwards' – at which point we see Flynn doing the same, scaling a castle wall to get to his enskied goal: a woman's bedroom. Yet what might seem to be a joke turns out to be solemnly earnest. Despite his antiquated costume, this Don Juan is an agent of current American foreign policy.

At the English court, he demands diplomatic access to Elizabeth I, wanting to ease relations with Spain and frustrate the warmongers at home. The analogy with international affairs in the 1930s and '40s is obvious; in Flynn's previous piratical escapades, Philip II had been an encoded Hitler. Returning to Madrid, Flynn laments its gloomy mood – 'no fun, no laughter!' The fault again is diagnosed according to American political values. The people are being taxed to extinction and press-ganged into the army by the Duke of Lorca, who's fomenting war for his personal gain. Flynn, of course, redresses grievances and, as he does so, evokes another of Don Juan's characters: Robin Hood. His conscience about social welfare leaves him little time for flirting, and any list he compiled would be featurelessly uniform. The girls who cluster round him are look-alike starlets, as identical as Busby Berkeley's battalions of chorines. Don Juan's mind is on professional advancement. He is commissioned in the Spanish navy, though pacifism overrules his ambition and he refuses the post, since he won't be part of the Armada against England.

Appointed fencing instructor at the Royal Academy, he matily volunteers to teach the sport to a dwarf. The Spanish Queen compliments him: 'You have made a friend.' Don Juan smarmily answers, 'I can use friends, Your Majesty.' From this American point of view, his catalogue is an exercise in how to win friends and influence people; the libertine is the world's most intrepid and bonus-laden travelling salesman. At another point in the film, Don Juan is swashbuckling with the villainous Lorca. The King interrupts, and orders him to throw down his sword. He does so at once, instinctively obedient.

The archetypal Don Giovanni doesn't even respect God, let alone a monarch. But, to our dismay this twentieth-century Don Juan has at last made good. When that occurs, his flame is extinguished. There's no more to be said about him.

Valmont – or the Marquise Unmasked

MARINA WARNER

Thirty years ago, various representatives of the French literary world tried to prevent Roger Vadim's 1959 film version of Laclos' novel *Les Liaisons dangereuses* from being shown, claiming it would bring the nation's *patrimoine* into disrepute. Today, Christopher Hampton's version of the novel, a huge draw on the London stage, has been adapted by him for the screen and become an even greater popular and critical sensation. Meanwhile Milos Forman has made another film version, called simply *Valmont*.[1] Laclos' Don Juan has become a hero of our time, and his courtship – of the public at least – continues unopposed.

The Vicomte de Valmont, Laclos' male seducer, is six years older than Mozart's Don Giovanni (the novel appeared in 1782).[2] Both meet the description of the legendary Don Juan as Camus saw him: an embodied principle of desire which in itself provokes desire.[3] He is irresistible, and his dangerous reputation does nothing to thwart his conquests: the objects of his attention are all aware of it, seek to escape from the danger, but cannot. Elvira knows, pursues, succumbs again – almost. As for Mme de Merteuil, it was Valmont's fame as a seducer that spurred her original longing for him (one of the planks of the legend is that all women secretly want to appear in Don Juan's catalogue of conquests). Like Don Giovanni, he is aristocratic, too, while his partner in crime Mme de Merteuil shares a title with Laclos' real-life contemporary and *vicieux*, the Marquis de Sade. The focus of all feminine susceptibilities, Valmont is himself impervious; always aroused, securely virile, he is never touched. At least, not until he meets his nemesis, in the form of the Marquise's implacable revenge for his surrender to a rival, the Présidente de Tourvel.

Valmont's discovery of love with Mme de Tourvel represents a significant difference between Da Ponte and Mozart's Don Giovanni and Laclos' seducer, and it makes Valmont a precursor of the hero of José Zorrillo's popular romantic play, *Don Juan Tenorio*, written in 1844 and still performed annually in Spain today. In this romance, Don Juan is saved by the love of the pure virgin Dona Iñes. But there are deeper points of contact and difference between Don Giovanni in the opera and Valmont in *Les Liaisons dangereuses*, as well as changed nuances of emphasis between the Laclos novel and the film version by Christopher Hampton. They reflect sharply current unease about sex and the state of play – of battle – in the bedroom; in short, the modern politics of seduction can be read therein.

In *Don Giovanni*, as in earlier, Spanish versions of the Don Juan story, women are the immediate objects of the hero's desire, but the ultimate targets of his exploits are men, the men who hold the women in their keeping: fathers, husbands, fiancés. In the first scene of the opera, Don Giovanni kills Donna Anna's father the Commendatore, who has been roused by her screams, and rushed to help her. Later, on the eve of her wedding, Zerlina presents a specially piquant challenge, and Masetto, her rustic bridegroom, an amusing prey. Donna Elvira, however, unhusbanded, unmanned, stalking her seducer on her own, puts him to flight; in her case, there is no male protector, no masculine ownership to defy and outdo. According to the code of *omertà* that obtained in southern Europe throughout the era of chivalry and into the modern period, a man's honour was kept by the women of his house, by the daughters, the wives, the sisters, and, not least, the mothers. They could plunge a family into bloodshed for centuries by their folly, ruin a brother, husband, or father by their lapses, or redeem him, as Dona Iñes does in Zorrillo's play, by their goodness. A man's standing in society, as well as his immortal soul, was in hostage to his womenfolk. But their accumulation of virtue was highly vulnerable to attack: it constituted a store which could be raided like any other goods, and its guardians were not all like Dona Iñes. Rather, like Eve, they were easily seduced, and the seducer, by robbing a man of his women's virtue, grew himself in reputation and stature as surely as if he had seized valuables of a material order. Don Giovanni allows us to glimpse, past the dazzle and high spirits of Mozart's *dramma giocoso*, this remorseless aristocratic economy, in which women are prizes at stake in a struggle for power between men.

Duelling is the inevitable consequence of such tension at the heart of Latin society: the violence by which Don Giovanni lives meets the violence with which first the Commendatore, then Don Ottavio, must defend Donna Anna. For every rapist, a knight errant; for every Don Juan, a Don Quixote. In fact, chivalrous males can do without women much more easily than without each other.

In *Les Liaisons dangereuses*, on the other hand, Valmont's manifest ambition focuses less clearly on the men behind the women; he is a thoroughgoing libertine, bent on pleasure and the sweets of power over women, especially resistant young maidens like Cécile Volanges, or honest wives, like Mme de Tourvel. But the Marquise de Merteuil performs with supreme art as a broker in men's honour: in her key letter (no. 81) when she analyses her methods to Valmont, she explains that she always extracts a secret from her lovers with which she can blackmail them, so that they can never unmask her and damage her honour. Her motive for debauching Cécile Volanges is revenge on the young woman's future husband; throughout the novel Laclos shows Merteuil gradually ensnaring and immobilizing Valmont himself as poisonously as the famed black widow spider. Her own male protectors dead, a widow without parents or children, she plays with women too, as does Don Juan, in order to humiliate and disempower men; she has taken up occupation of a masculine place in the code of chivalry, and her scheming and pursuits seem in the novel all the more diabolical for this trespass across the boundaries of gender.

But what appeared unwomanly and anomalous, even fiendish, in the eighteenth century does not strike the present-day reader in the same light. The economics of chivalry have changed, and with them the objectives of seduction. Don Giovanni, with his Faustian heroics against fathers, law-givers, husbands, does not speak to our times as clearly as Valmont and Madame de Merteuil's partnership. With their different erotic objectives, the protagonists of *Les Liaisons dangereuses* reflect the business of sex today with more hardheadedness. For the Marquise, men are the paramount antagonists, including the Vicomte she cherishes so deeply for his villainy. When he offers her an ultimatum, demanding that she keep her word and reward him with a night in her bed, she hurls the curt message at him, 'Eh bien, la guerre.' In the cinema, we expect from her half-smile that she will surrender to Valmont's eager charms, and her duellist's challenge (again, a masculine impulse) makes an effective *coup de théâtre*.

In this twentieth-century movie of the Don Juan myth, the woman on her own is no longer the piteous raving Elvira, driven to love and to save, to denounce the beloved seducer and then yield to him all over again, but a malignant and frozen sensualist who has learned never to confuse sex and love, the pleasures of love and the lover himself. Christopher Hampton had already translated Molière's *Dom Juan*, in 1974. He once commented on the Molière: 'the harsh moral of his rigorous fable rings as true today as it ever has: if you let yourself be fucked, you will be . . .' His consciousness of the timeliness of such studies in cold-hearted eroticism may well have led him on to consider Laclos' novel, and in his skilful synthesis of a long book, Hampton pauses to dramatize the important moment of self-revelation on the Marquise's part, when she describes how she steeled herself to survive:

I practised detachment. I learned how to look cheerful, while under the table I stuck a fork into the back of my hand. I became a virtuoso of deceit. It wasn't pleasure I was after, it was knowledge. I consulted the strictest moralists to learn how to appear, philosophers to find out what to think and novelists to see what I could get away with. And, in the end, I distilled everything down to one wonderfully simple principle: win or die.[4]

There is an apparent feminist edge to the Marquise's declaration, which the film script seizes, and on which the actress, Glenn Close, builds. In Laclos, the Marquise characterizes herself as a Delilah, avenging her sex for the boredom and imprisonment inflicted on it by men ('Née pour venger mon sexe et maîtriser le vôtre . . .', she writes). In the film, the Marquise repudiates men as thoroughly as in the book, freezing out Valmont for his 'marital tone' when he tries to order her about. But she never adduces chivalry towards her own sex as a motive. In the 1980s, survival in the battle seems reason enough for her conduct.

A woman on her own, if determined not to capitulate to the seductions or the commandments of the male, has to find a *raison d'être*, or have one found for her by her creators. Mozart's opera proposes passion for vengeance in Elvira; Laclos presents Merteuil as unnatural, a monstrous usurper of a male sexuality. But Hampton, viewing the Marquise from the vantage-point of today, finds something natural in her reaction to her female predicament. The film's choice of a Versailles-like *palais de glaces*, a hall of mirrors, for the Marquise's apartments, points up her poker game of feints and illusion, the narcissism in the seducer's exercise of power, but it also stirs other associations. As long ago as 1929, the psychoanalyst Joan Rivière offered a depressing, influential insight into the changing character of sexual engagement since emancipation. Womanliness itself, she proposes, has become a masquerade.[5] Rivière, inspired by her clinical studies, was writing about the 'new career woman', and noted, 'Not long ago intellectual pursuits for women were associated almost exclusively with an overtly masculine type of woman who, in pronounced cases, made no secret of her wish or claim to be a man. This has now changed.' Rivière went on to discuss one case history and described a performance of femininity, a 'masquerade' of compulsive twittering and coquetting. Glenn Close, playing the Marquise de Merteuil, is surrounded by mirrors, in which her perfected toilette and elaborate ornaments are continually refracted; schooling herself not to register her feelings on her face, practising detachment as fervently as a stylite, she is engaged in a lifelong masquerade too, because she has not been able to live openly the independent way she wanted, nor achieve her ends except by pretending to be a different kind of creature, a conventional woman, without appetite or intelligence, uninterested in sexual satisfaction or other power.

However, the film's sympathies with its evil genius only go so far: it would be reading against the text to invite compassion when the Marquise is publicly shamed at the Opéra. In the stage version, Hampton chose not to punish her so publicly and dramatically at the end, diverging from Laclos, who banishes her from society, and then disfigures her with smallpox. The playwright may have avoided the book's morality-tale ending in the stage version because it seemed too pat. If Mme de Merteuil's individual and extreme wickedness is wholly to blame, then the contemporary reverberations he had set in motion about her situation would go for nothing.

Some of the other changes to the novel in its journey from play to film tend to play down the glimmerings of sympathy for women's erotic life that *Les Liaisons dangereuses* can at times inspire. In *Dangerous Liaisons*, the director Stephen Frears follows Valmont's point of view more often than Merteuil's: Merteuil is more often beheld rather than the eyes through which we are watching and understanding the action. Within her masquerade, she remains to a great extent concealed from us too. It is Valmont, played by John Malkovich, who becomes the presiding consciousness of the film.

Valmont differs from his peer, Don Giovanni, in obvious ways: for one thing, he scores success after success, unlike Mozart's hero, who is comically checked at every turn. Also Valmont sometimes undertakes his seductions because he is told to by the Marquise; his pursuit of her, and his frustrated desire to renew their lost liaison effectively provide a motive for most of the mischief in the plot. Like the legendary Don Juan, however, he is not to blame for the passions women excite in him; a Don Juan, as Ovid made clear in *The Art of Loving*, is God's gift to women, only giving them what they want:

A man who kisses a girl and goes no further deserves to forfeit even the pleasure of kissing her. Obviously one wants to do a great deal more than that, and if one does not, one is being, not civilized, but silly.

'Oh, but I should hate to use brute force,' you say. Why, that is exactly what girls like: they often prefer to enjoy themselves under duress. The victim of a sexual assault is generally delighted, for she takes your audacity as a compliment; whereas the girl who could have been raped but was not is bound to feel disappointed . . .[6]

It is a principle of the myth of the eternal seducer that the raped are ravished by untold pleasure; the male fantasy in *Les Liaisons dangereuses* develops it further, and shows the needs of women generously met not only by Valmont's prowess in bed (Cécile, raped, becomes an apt and lusty pupil) but by his submission to the Marquise's machinations, and prolonged obedience to the imperative of his frustrated desire for her. The necessary simplification of the novel for the cinema also points up a central, contemporary twist in the interpretation of the two protagonists' relationship, which twitches aside another mask from the Marquise, to reveal how she is beheld by the chief man in her life:

MERTEUIL: We loved each other once, didn't we? I think it was love. And you made me very happy.
VALMONT: And I could again. We just untied the knot, it was never broken.
MERTEUIL: Illusions, of course, are by their nature sweet.
VALMONT: I have no illusions. I lost them on my travels. Now I want to come home.[7]

The rake wants to come home.

Is this a meeting of husband and wife after a separation? Surely Merteuil's enmity towards marriage, surpassing even the traditional aversion of the professional seducer, must rule out an understanding that the pair are nostalgic for connubial bliss. No, in the late 1980s, when the rake asks to come home, he is not talking to a beloved mistress or a forsaken wife, but rather to another woman in his life – his mother.

Don Juan has no mother. Don Giovanni has no mother either, only a father figure: Elvira, Dona Iñes and other women who have loved, forgiven and redeemed the rake fulfil a kind of maternal function in the legend, as intercessors for his salvation, like the Virgin Mary in early versions of the Don Juan legend, miracle stories about the deathbed repentance of daredevils and rascals. But Laclos shadows forth another kind of mothering in the famous seducer's life when he creates his monstrous Marquise, and Hampton caught his drift and rendered visible the invisible mother of Don Juan in the form of Mme de Merteuil: a perverted Phaedra, a cold-blooded Clytemnestra, Hamlet's mother Gertrude and Snow White's wicked Queen looking at themselves in mirrors.

To see Merteuil as Valmont's mother does not entail reading the novel itself, and its current avatars, as essentially Oedipal; nor agreeing with some interpreters who have analysed the whole Don Juan complex in those terms. (The Errol Flynn vehicle, written by a woman – Bess Meredyth – in 1926, provides the only instance I've come across of Don Juan's mother appearing in the story: she's caught *in flagrante* and harshly repudiated by little Juan's father, who then sternly warns the boy against all women, setting him on a lifelong quest for true love.) But listening to that odd filial note, 'Now I want to come home,' does deepen the realization that the misogynist aspects in the Freudian analysis of male sexuality inform the understanding and representation of female sexuality today. The mother shows her Medusa face and scares the little boy into manliness, despatching him into the world outside the home, enabling him to turn his desire towards other women besides herself, and so further the existence of human society: in other words, his desire lies in her gift, at her command, arising from fear of the castration she inspires. (So orthodoxy would have it.) It seems to me that this is a model of sexual struggle that is becoming more widely and unquestioningly acknowledged, as women express themselves strongly about their needs and wants, and men fail to develop a correspondingly articulate rebellion against the traditional perception of male desire as rampant, unfocused, violent, threatening and threatened. Somewhere, in the midst of the initial struggle going on about the character of maleness, the character of femaleness, a huge new population of fantasy females – hard women, sadistic specialists, phallic mothers – has grown, most obviously in the pornography industry, but also, pervasively, in other branches of entertainment and culture. The bridle that women were supposed to extend to their mates, according to Victorian models of sexuality, in order to tame and harness them, has become a goad, and a pretext for a renewed, but different, masculine claim that responsibility for male sexuality lies with the female.

This shift of the sexual burden, from men to women, can be seen through a comparison of *Don Giovanni* with Stephen Frears' film *Dangerous Liaisons*. In the opera, the entirely masculine figure of the Commendatore, father of Anna, embodies the law the libertine flouts. He has even been identified with Mozart's own father, who died while Mozart was composing the opera. A military commander transformed into a stone statue, he incorporates the values of solidity and rectitude and constancy and strength that the Don has rejected on his heedless whirl of changing partners and broken promises. The archetypal Don Juan, apostate and blasphemer, defies God the Father and his commandments and all his earthly representatives; *Le Festin de pierre*, an early dramatic version of the legend in France (1652/9), was actually subtitled 'Le Fils criminel'. Don Giovanni kills the Commendatore, defies his ghost, refuses to repent when he appears at the final banquet and is instead hurled down into hell. In a reversal of 'Là ci darem la mano', when he was wooing Zerlina with false promises, he takes the Commendatore's hand in good faith – and, for the first time, he himself tastes betrayal.

Mozart's Don Giovanni quickly became a hero of Romanticism precisely because he is so headstrong, seizing what is forbidden – sex – at the risk to his own life and soul. He dares be a man when the divine law denies him his instincts, and embraces his death. To the Romantics, his rebellion was magnificent, the divine authority of the patriarch could prevail over his body, but not his spirit; the opera ends with Don Giovanni's heroism exalted and purified by his damnation. He's the Faust who does not regret the pact with the Devil because he exults in his knowledge, he's Adam and Eve refusing to despair after the Fall, for they prefer mortality to Eden, human experience to perfect bliss.

Valmont also meets his death, at the hands of the Chevalier Danceny. He repents too, but betrays the Marquise with his last breath, one of his rare excursions into truthful utterance. He seals her fate, as assuredly as killing her. Just as the law is embodied by the Commendatore, so Valmont's law is laid down by the Marquise: though they claim to be equal allies, he is the tool of her intrigues and when he departs from her wishes, as in the case of Mme de Tourvel, becomes the target of her vengeance. Valmont is driven by her in a more straightforward manner than Don Giovanni is ruled by the Commendatore, and the shift from a prevailing male dynamic to a female one is a significant aspect of the contemporary revival of interest in Laclos' novel.

Don Juan is usually portrayed as needlessly self-willed; his drive to defy the patriarch does not provide an open reason for his conduct. In fact, he rarely offers a motive at all. As embodied desire, he merely acts, follows his nose, literally flaring the 'odor di femmina' on the air, a god liberated from the rules that govern mortal relations, as free to ravish as Jove himself. His 'mad pursuit', as Keats described the rape on the Grecian urn, only leads on to more, madder pursuits; Don Giovanni exults, during the 'champagne aria', his only extended solo in the opera, on the increase in his score, like a speculator contemplating a killing in the market. The music and the words imitate his stock-taking by their redoubled repeats:

> 'con questa e quella vo amoreggiar
> vo amoreggiar amoreggiar
> Ah, la mia lista, doman mattina
> d'una decina devi aumentar.'

Molière's Don Juan also acts on his own, wilfully flouting the received code of conduct and airing his views so thoroughly in the course of the play that he has little time left over – on stage – for flirtations; agnostic defiance, rationalism, anti-clericalism, and a characteristic Molièrian repugnance for humbug animate his declared lust. Here, the century before Mozart and Da Ponte, the chief mortal sin in the eyes of the church – concupiscence – becomes the chief weapon of dissent. Molière's Don Juan speaks for the seventeenth-century enlightenment, and succeeded too well in his challenge: the play was banned.

The rebel character of the hero made him a pattern of Romanticism: a loner, a kind of suicide, a saint of love and the personal quest for knowledge, whose final incarnation perhaps was Genêt, seen through the eyes of Sartre. Although Valmont also finds love and damnation and death in the course of Laclos' novel, he could not become, with Don Govanni, a fully fledged Romantic hero during the nineteenth century, because Laclos' pious intentions deny Valmont full responsibility for his actions. Don Giovanni is magnificent in his autonomy, his loneliness: he resembles the solitary watcher on the promontory or the wanderer in the forest of Caspar David Friedrich's paintings from the decades following the opera; he sins, and takes the consequences. In *Les Liaisons dangereuses*, it is Mme de Merteuil who takes the rap. Although her malice is hypnotizing to the reader as well as to Valmont, her culpability ultimately diminishes the novel. The workings of desire in *Don Giovanni* magnify a struggle about carnality we all intuit within ourselves (regardless of gender), even if we are spared it in experience. But Mme de Merteuil is a special case, and Laclos' notion of blame a cowardly one. When Valmont parrots to Mme de Tourvel the farewell letter the Marquise has produced, he uses the gallic shrug to devastating effect:

'Adieu, mon ange, je t'ai prise avec plaisir; je te quitte sans regret: je te reviendrai peut-être. Ainsi va le monde.'

Then he repeats once more the refrain, with which he has closed each line of this death sentence:

'Ce n'est pas ma faute.'

Cynicism about human nature and about society inspire him, he tells her. The original sin which drives Don Giovanni has become, in the world of *Les Liaisons*, a form of social mores. Though Mme de Merteuil and Valmont are both using languid pessimism as a weapon against the Présidente de Tourvel's pathetic struggle to be good, the novel still makes it clear that Mme de Merteuil, like the Tempter in the original miracle stories, not only whispers Valmont's misdeeds and then spurs him on, but, just like Satan, is fully cognisant of her own wickedness, and content. She has taken the place of Mephistopheles in the prototype of Faust, the tale of Theophilus who sold his soul to the Devil for a bishopric, but was saved by the Virgin Mary.

Between the page and the screen, something has changed this notoriously pitiless missive of Valmont to Mme de Tourvel. Hampton has translated Valmont's refrain 'Ce n'est pas ma faute' (simply, 'It's not my fault') to 'It's beyond my control.'

The scene when he renounces the Présidente is still horrifying, and Malkovich manages to convey how his words clash with his inner feelings more sensitively than fidelity to the book would call for. But this throws even more responsibility on to Merteuil, as does the phrase 'beyond my control'. 'Fault' is a general concept, roughly referring to the weakness of all men; 'ce n'est pas ma faute' is a coward's excuse, but it emanates from the same universe where Don Giovanni stands and defends the human against the divine judge, where men are possessed by lust and cannot do otherwise. (It has little to do, however, with Molière's hero's world, in which he alone elects, through reason, to follow the path he has chosen.) Mme de Merteuil, by contrast, filtered through Hampton's script and acted by Glenn Close, a star famous for performances in rawly violent films about sex (*Jagged Edge*, *Fatal Attraction*) is a contemporary creation for these times of sexual drive and purpose and independence; yet her relation to the principal man in her life is best characterized as incestuous. She goads him to perform, she delights in his success (but not so that he notices and slackens off), she defends her right to entertain a young lover in the face of his disapproval and jealousy, but her possessiveness leads her to cut him off when he falls in love, because she will accept no rival in his attachments. The power she has over him is convincing to modern eyes, both in the novel and in the cinema because it matches a recognizable and widespread power of women, one that is not forbidden to them: maternal authority. Her responsibility for his sexual exploits becomes acceptable too, for the same reason. Glenn Close herself hardly looks depraved, cruel, or sexually unscrupulous, whereas John Malkovich has sensually vulpine and sardonic features, perfectly expressive of Valmont's acid eroticism. But it is a tenet of the new, mythologized female sexuality that even the coolest, blandest, and most cerebral of women can be possessed of insatiable desires which will impel them to stop at nothing in their hunger for gratification. Hence the casting of Glenn Close in the 1980s; in the late 1950s, the choice fell on the convincingly night-prowling Jeanne Moreau.

The post-Freudian dispensation draws us into pinning blame on women (and on Mother, above all) in a different way from before, and *Dangerous Liaisons* illustrates how: no one would now claim, with Ovid, that Valmont's victims were begging for it really, but many accept thoughtlessly that a man can remain under a woman's control like a small boy, and in the name of the 'phallic mother', locate the springs of masculine action in female authority. This particular form of the Don Juan myth holds sway now partly because it still seduces women themselves as well as men: motherhood is a site of female power and a legitimate social role which allows needs and desires to be expressed aloud. It is today's masquerade, the permitted face of woman, like the flirtatiousness of the 1920s, to which Rivière referred. The tyranny Mme de Merteuil exercises over Valmont can be thrilling to women, as much as Don Giovanni's boldness. (At the age of sixteen or seventeen, when I first read the novel, I too wanted that power, in kind and degree.) But one has to take care with this type of lure: a fantasy of control will always seduce the disenfranchised. (Unemployed teenagers wear combat fatigues and gigantic boots; prostitutes solicit business by boasting of their dominatrix methods.) This is perhaps the final twist in the seductions of Don Juan, that the victims are flattered into believing themselves in charge.

Don Giovanni hurls his challenge to women, principle, convention, sincerity and death itself, and finds that his life spins out of his control. As Don Giovanni plunges into the flames at the end of Mozart's opera, the three women sing like accomplices in his undoing, like the Moirae themselves: they have survived. Yet the closing triumphal sextet of the *dramma giocoso* hardly leaves us with a morbid image of the power of women or their responsibility for what has occurred. *Les Liaisons dangereuses*, on the other hand, reveals a preying mantis universe in which men and women engage to the death, committed alike to destruction and self-destruction. At the end of the novel, the saintly Madame de Tourvel is dead, Cécile Volanges shut in a convent, and the Marquise imprisoned behind her ruined beauty; all varieties of closure that also strip disguises from the three women, and effectively put an end to pretences and dissimulation – and to seduction and sex.

The book's moral, which the film grippingly expands in a contemporary mode, offers a clammy warning in an age of material extravagance, conspicuous hedonism, sexual emancipation, AIDS, and deep anxiety about the place of sex in love. The compensations of such pessimism are obvious, and in some way similar to the surface satisfactions offered by Don Giovanni's come-uppance ('that's what you get'). But the fatal female libertine commanding the debauches of the male has returned as a compelling figure today because she embodies a contemporary fantasy about women's sexual domination and responsibility for men's desire. When Valmont looks at himself in the glass, he always sees the Marquise at his ear, urging him to do better. Every age gets the Don Juan it deserves; Valmont is the face of Don Giovanni for our time.

Notes

1 Not released in England at the time of writing.

2 I've used the Garnier edition of the novel by Choderlos de Laclos, Yves Le Hir (ed.) (Paris, 1961).

3 Albert Camus, 'Le Don Juanisme' in *Le Mythe de Sisyphe* (Paris, 1942), pp. 97–106.

4 Christopher Hampton, *Dangerous Liaisons: the film* (Faber, 1989), p. 26.

5 Joan Rivière, 'Womanliness as a masquerade', in *Formations of Fantasy*, Victor Burgin, James Donald and Cora Kaplan (eds.) (London, 1986), p. 35. See Stephen Heath, 'Joan Rivière and the Masquerade', ibid. pp. 46–61.

6 Ovid, *The Technique of Love*, trans. Paul Turner (London, 1968), p. 46.

7 Hampton, op. cit., p. 56.

Reading Don Giovanni

JOSEPH KERMAN

I

Mozart's Don Giovanni – the man, not the opera – is one thing
and the Don Juan idea, myth, or archetype is another kind of
thing altogether: though each is unthinkable without the other.
Mozart himself and his poet, Lorenzo Da Ponte, would not have
spoken of a myth, of course. But they were well aware of the long
tradition of Don Juan depictions preceding their own; this
anyone would assume, even without knowing that Da Ponte, in
writing his text, helped himself liberally to another on the same
subject, by the librettist Giovanni Bertati. Bertati, in turn, refers
ironically to the myth in its essential stage tradition. (The
prologue of his opus is about a theatrical company in financial
straits, deciding reluctantly to mount a show that will appeal to
the lowest common denominator – a Don Juan play. Bertati's
version of this follows.) As sophisticated men of letters, Bertati
and Da Ponte knew Don Juans by Molière, Goldoni, and others,
which they drew upon in ways that scholars have traced with
exemplary thoroughness. Da Ponte also knew that in the sophisticated Vienna of his own time, an improvised Don Juan play was
mounted every year in the Octave of All Saints: a sort of
Josephine Rocky Horror Show.

So much for Mozart's time; *our* own time offers myriad sources
with which to expand or boggle one's mind about Mozart's Don
Giovanni. There are Don Juans by Byron, Shaw, and John
Berger, disquisitions on Don Juan by Kierkegaard, Reich, and

Camus, as well as quite voluminous writings by musicologists and critics that are less brilliant, no doubt, but certainly not without insight. The question is, perhaps, how much of this we need for whatever our purposes or interests may be. And if our primary interest is in Mozart's Don Giovanni, how much do we need to read into him? Why should we 'read' Don Giovanni in any other way than by attending closely and deeply to the opera's text? Giovanni is marvellously moulded by Mozart's music, even though he is also circumscribed by it (he is even circumscribed by Da Ponte's libretto). He would not seem to stand in need of support or sustenance from Don Juan.

In fact, Don Juan needs Don Giovanni more. As Bernard Williams points out in a devastatingly sensible recent article,[1] modern thought about Don Juan has been dominated by Mozart's embodiment of the myth:

> This is not merely because the opera is by far the greatest work given to this theme. It is also because the opera is in various ways problematical, and that it raises in a challenging way the question of what the figure of Giovanni means. Hence, not only is the opera the historical starting-point of many modern thoughts on this subject, but some of those thoughts lead directly back to the problem of understanding the opera itself.

Fair enough. But let us be clear about the concreteness and vitality of *Don Giovanni* at the present, in numerous productions by directors who refuse to be circumscribed. Don Juan, on the other hand, is now little more than an abstract idea left over from the past, awaiting an occasional new embodiment. Berger called his Don Juan novel *G*, not *J*.

This was perhaps already the situation in the time of Søren Kierkegaard, who, Williams reminds us, first brought together three central facts about *Don Giovanni*: 'that the opera is of great and unsettling power, that a seducer is at the centre of it, and that the seducer is virtually characterless'. These facts provided Kierkegaard with a springboard for philosophizing about art and the erotic and the idea of Don Juan. Thinking about these same central facts in the light of Mozart's music can also help us read Don Giovanni.

II

There are two ways of viewing the picture that Mozart and Da Ponte have drawn of Don Giovanni as a seducer. One way takes the authors as ironists. This view is memorialized in a throwaway from Edward Dent's marvellous old book on Mozart's operas – a book which is probably still too influential on English Mozartians. 'Busoni used to say that Don Giovanni was the man who gave every woman the supreme experience of happiness,' wrote Dent, who was also a biographer and a great admirer of Busoni. Yet 'if his adventures within the limited period of the opera are a fair sample, he has no success at all and is placed in a completely ridiculous situation every time'.[2] The point that Giovanni's actions as set forth in the drama matter more than reportage by the envious, such as that in Leporello's Catalogue Aria, must be granted – an obvious point, perhaps, but one that it is just as well to have made.

The other way takes Mozart and Da Ponte as realists. Given the conditions of theatrical censorship at the time, it can be maintained that they have presented a picture of the seducer that is remarkably penetrating and unvarnished. *Bist du nicht willig, so brauch' ich Gewalt*; Don Giovanni as a seducer runs the gamut from persuasion to force. His first scene, which shapes our impression of him unforgettably, is an interrupted rape. His last seduction – his serenade to Elvira's maid – involves only suasion or cajolement. (This scene, however, besides being highly forgettable in dramatic terms, is conceptually bizarre. For in the deepest sense an opera character who does not sing does not exist, and this maid does not sing, nor even appear. No wonder the outcome of this mild seduction, or indeed anything else about it, remains unmentioned during the rest of the opera.)

The seduction of Zerlina – the only one that the opera treats at any length – shows explicitly how, in the seducer/rapist's transactions, violence is implicated with persuasion. On their first encounter, Don Giovanni does even less than cajole, in my apprehension of 'Là ci darem la mano'; he is going through the motions knowing that he already has the green light. If we are encouraged to think of Zerlina's *sposo* as a premature *sansculotte*, we can hardly conceive of her as some kind of Arcadian shepherdess who believes Giovanni when he says he will marry her. She and Giovanni both have one thing in mind – an 'innocente amor', as they call it later, innocent of violence or partiality.

So she tells him what he wants to hear, and he sings to her in the same spirit. Zerlina acknowledges Giovanni right away by singing his tune. All he has to do is set down the simplest of melodic building blocks; it is Zerlina who ornaments the famous melody, plays with it (and with Giovanni), extends it, and so on. Despite her show of tremulousness, she is fully in control. When Giovanni whispers 'Andiam, andiam' (let us go), moving gently higher and higher up through the scale degrees, Zerlina answers all by herself, on cue. When she sings 'Andiam' on the dominant – that is, when the matter is officially decided – Giovanni doesn't even have to sing along.

Their second encounter is quite different, of course; Don Giovanni does not so much cajole Zerlina as push her. This is near the beginning of the Act I finale. Zerlina is upset because Masetto is watching, but a new plangency in the music indicates also that she now wants nothing to do with the seducer. Her chromatic appoggiaturas no longer sound pert, but painful; her tremulous semiquavers, if not quite frantic, are rushed and squeezed by comparison with 'Là ci darem'. (Compare 'non *son* più forte, non *son* più forte, non *son* più forte' in the earlier scene with 'Ah, lasciatemi andar *vi*a!', 'Se pietade avete in *co*re', and '. . . far, so ben io, so ben io . . .' in the later one.) As for the third encounter between Giovanni and Zerlina, that is recorded later in the finale by an off-stage scream.

The history of this seduction, then, traces a sequence from play to pressure to assault. By extrapolation back to the Anna episode, and then forward to the end of the opera, the seducer's progress is shown to proceed from play to rape and murder, and from there to hellfire.

If with Zerlina what is developed in the opera is her actual seduction, with the other two women what is developed is the psychological damage occasioned by the seducer/rapist's ministrations. By the end of the opera, both Donna Anna and Donna Elvira are broken women. Many things are echoed twice in the dramatic structure of *Don Giovanni*, but only one thing happens, excruciatingly, three times: the humiliation of Elvira by Giovanni in front of his servant. On the last occasion, as Wye Jamison Allanbrook remarks, Giovanni's 'dining-salon has become a private limbo in which all three characters are eternally joined in barren but immutable relation'.[3] 'Alone at the final curtain, she will have no future', writes Lawrence Lipking. 'The violence done to her illusions has brought her to a sort of posthumous existence, in which she is conscious of the futility of her hopes even when acting them out.'

Donna Anna, in traumatized response to the opera's opening string of events, expresses herself in an accompanied recitative and a duet which are among the opera's most powerful, most radical, and greatest numbers. Still splendid as she sings 'Or sai chi l'onore', she becomes a shadowed figure thereafter. The effect of her short entry speech in the Act III sextet, 'Lascia almen alla mia pena', is of a single, piercing glimpse of anguish;[4] for better or for worse, it is Ottavio who is given the opportunity to dilate upon his feelings in this part of the opera (in the aria 'Il mio tesoro'). Her own opportunity, near the end of the action, has received a sharply divided press. Anna's big aria 'Non mi dir' impressed Berlioz for its 'intense sadness, full of a heartbreaking sense of loss and sorrowing love', but Berlioz's outrage at Anna's coloratura later in the aria rankled till the end of his life ('one of the most odious crimes against passion, taste, and common sense of which the history of art provides an example'). The piece has seemed 'singularly cold and unemotional' to Dent, and – which is not the same thing – 'chilling' to so sympathetic a recent commentator as Allanbrook. Certainly Anna's final music – the little duet in which she puts off her wedding to Ottavio – is of stupendous vacuity.

We first see Donna Anna as a woman of formidable courage, pride, purpose, and, by the way, physical strength. When we last see and hear her she is a shell of her former self. She is Mozart's most cruel and painful portrait.

III

'An opera of great and unsettling power', says Bernard Williams. Unsettling, and powerfully so: because the work is manifestly problematic and tension-filled, and also because in some ways it can make a modern audience really uncomfortable. Lipking says as much in his discussion of the audience's enforced voyeurism of the *donna abbandonata*, and I have my own furtive list of things that perturb. George Bernard Shaw, who published his first dramas under the ironic title *Plays Pleasant and Unpleasant*, would not have applied the latter adjective to *Man and Superman*, his own contribution to the Don Juan–Don Giovanni crux. But I think of *Don Giovanni* itself as Mozart's unpleasant opera.

One reason is its repeated representation of cruelty: not only psychological cruelty, such as has been discussed to some extent above, but also low-level sadism. Leporello has to whistle with his mouth full as he waits on table, sidestep a rapier in the graveyard, and dodge a thrashing such as Masetto actually suffers. Even Zerlina figuratively bears her backside to Masetto (as well as her breast); and if we have read in Dent that 'Batti, batti' refers to a then-recent scandal in which a Venetian doctor stripped a gentlewoman and flagellated her publicly on the Fondamenta della Tana, singing a vulgar song, the aria becomes distinctly unappetizing. Audiences have more or less cheerfully inured themselves to such staples of earthy humour. (They have drawn the line, thank heaven, at the Razor Duet, 'Fra queste due mannine', which was added by Mozart to the second, Viennese performance but is seldom performed today – though there are directors who might enjoy Zerlina's symbolic castration of Leporello in his role as Giovanni-surrogate. The other additions to the second performance, Ottavio's 'Dalla sua pace' and Elvira's 'Quali eccessi, o numi' – 'Mi tradì quell'alma ingrata', have entered the opera's canonic text.)

The opera is also unsettling because of its wild contrasts of tone and style. These stem from a much-debated generic crux. Da Ponte called *Don Giovanni* a *'dramma giocoso'*, a recognized theatrical genre of the time which sought to fuse elements of *opera seria* and *opera buffa*. The same genre title was used by Bertati. Yet fusion seems to have been far from Mozart's mind. Donna Anna and Don Ottavio, the *opera seria* characters who promote so much of the action, nevertheless float above it, carrying out a desperate private inner action of their own. Tight-lipped, they sometimes allow Donna Elvira to come along – she is the so-called *'mezza carattere'* role, mediating between *seria* and *buffa* – but they cannot and never do acknowledge the existence of the *opera buffa* peasant pair. Although they occasionally address Masetto and Zerlina in *secco* recitative, their concerted music never engages. Ottavio's arias are notorious for their withdrawal from the opera's essential concerns, and this quality also explains why his confrontation with Giovanni in the Act I finale is so blank. It is not so much that Giovanni brazens the situation out, escapes, whatever. It is rather that he and Ottavio cannot engage within a single field of action.

There is one place of genuine engagement, to be sure, in the opera's indelible opening scene. Here Anna not only addresses Giovanni but engages with him physically, struggles with him. It is a problematic scene, as I shall suggest later, and the problem is compounded by the shock of generic violation. The genres do not fuse, they fight.

What is more, another genre is fighting to get out here – continuous opera: that is, opera in which the singing is continuously backed by fully developed orchestral music, rather than switching in and out of stretches of low-level talk presented in *secco* recitative. This was, as we know, the operatic wave of the future. Mozart must have known, too – from works he had encountered by Gluck – though the closest he himself had come to writing continuous opera was in the long sectional finales to

Acts II and IV of *Le nozze di Figaro*. All Mozartian opera is conducted on two sharply different imaginative levels, one defined by orchestral music and the other by a rudimentary, sub- or semi-musical framework of speech or *secco* recitative, accompanied only by harpsichord and a single cello. The great *Figaro* finales come at the end of scenes which begin in this 'stop-and-go' mode, but which end as forecasts of continuous opera.

Before *Don Giovanni*, however, Mozart had never arranged for a long sectional finale actually to coincide with a whole scene, curtain to curtain. Now, when the curtain goes up on the opera's last scene, we hear continuous orchestral music and no *secco* recitative whatsoever until it goes down. The Act II finale is a virtuoso exercise in musical linkage involving nine distinct sections or 'movements'. The fact of continuity itself gives the scene an immediacy that was not available to any of the traditional eighteenth-century operatic genres – even apart from the particulars of Mozart's composition.

Something like this continuity, and this immediacy, exists across the opera's entire opening scene, too. The Overture leads directly (and consequentially) into the opera's first number, the sectional Act I Introduction; the end of this Introduction is not syntactically closed (has no final cadence) prior to a hasty *secco* recitative for Giovanni and Leporello; when Donna Anna returns, the same musical figure which ended the non-cadencing Introduction returns to initiate her accompanied recitative; and her duet with Ottavio emerges from that accompanied recitative seamlessly, again without punctuation. Technically speaking, the most radical feature here is the reactivation, in Anna's recitative, of the orchestra that had been suspended at the end of the Introduction. By this means Mozart contrived to include *secco* recitative within a compelling larger continuity, encompassing the entire scene.

This impressive and prescient essay in continuous opera is capped only by the opera's final scene, the giant continuous Act II finale mentioned above. It seems clear that these two special measures were taken in concert, because – in an unprecedented gesture – Mozart binds the two sections together musically.

Segments of music from the Andante of the Overture and from the duel are recapitulated with a devastating effect for the Commendatore's arrival to supper and his browbeating of Don Giovanni, respectively. The Act I opening complex goes from D minor to D major to D minor; the Act II finale goes from D major to D minor to D major.

All this was done, surely, with the express intention of holding together a notoriously scrappy piece of dramatic construction. There is really no reason to doubt that Mozart, who was a dramatic genius as well as a musical genius, understood the problem that he was faced with by Da Ponte's cobbled-up libretto. He devised his own radical way of dealing with it, a strictly musical way. In opera, the dramatist is the composer.

It is late in this essay to say what everyone knows, that *Don Giovanni* is full of brilliant and beautiful music. It is also known that *Don Giovanni*, more than Mozart's other great operas, also contains patches that are less than brilliant or beautiful. One can tire of Leporello's Catalogue Aria; 'Madamina' lacks the musical distinction of (say) the corresponding *basso buffo* aria in *Le nozze di Figaro*, Bartolo's 'La vendetta'. Elvira's 'Ah, fuggi il traditor', a puzzling and ineffective piece, in the last century was often cut. Anna's 'Non mi dir' is problematic even for some of its admirers. There are dead spots in both the Act I and Act II finales. Though its ontological status is unclear – does it exact our attention as part of an 'authentic' Viennese version of the opera? – there is also the exceptionally weak Razor Duet.

Of course the dead spot in the Act II finale comes only at the end, and 'goes to show how drab life is without the Don'. Of course Mozart understood – and wanted us to know – that Leporello the cataloguer is a hollow man compared to Bartolo, who in the Act III sextet of *Figaro* positively (if momentarily) glows with humanity. 'Non mi dir', I have said, is sung by a broken woman . . . and so on. It is very uncomfortable for a critic, even nerve-wracking, to have to keep arguing in this way. One wants to say instead: obviously the dramatic construction is scrappy at many points; the piece is constantly threatening to fly apart, since Mozart did not always attempt to patch it on the spot.

Instead he determined to bind the whole thing together on the highest level. The scrappiness of the plot and the binding created by the music – by the two continuous outer scenes with their musical echoes – go together.

This was an extraordinary conception, but also a scary one. Part of what makes *Don Giovanni* so unsettling is the sense – the teasing sense – that Mozart is going out of control. Actually this is not so: whether in spite of or because of its problematic nature, the piece always plays. But the tension in it between the dramatically centrifugal and the centripetal is practically palpable. *Don Giovanni* is a notoriously unclassical piece.

IV

Three central facts about *Don Giovanni* are 'that the opera is of great and unsettling power, that a seducer is at the centre of it, and that the seducer is virtually characterless'. Although Giovanni 'is in a deep way the life of the opera', as Bernard Williams puts it,

> such character as he has is not really as grand as that implies: he expresses more than he is. He seems to have no depth adequate to the work in which he plays the central role. He has, in a sense, a character – to a considerable extent a bad one. But we are not given any deep insight into what he really is, or what drives him on. We could not have been: it is not that there is something hidden in his soul. It is notable that he has no self-reflective aria – he never sings about himself, as Mozart's other central characters do.[5]

How are we to read this No-Man, as Wye Allanbrook persists in calling him? For 'read' read 'hear' – the caution is not redundant in this context.

We have to hear him in his famous Act I aria, the invincibly effective 'Fin ch'han dal vino'. If not self-reflective, this aria is certainly self-expressive, and deserves, perhaps, fairly close attention. The only possible trouble with the piece is its hectic velocity, its tendency to stun. It clocks in at just about eighty seconds; Don Giovanni sings at full tilt continuously, save for one two-bar rest which allows him a big gulp of air (or champagne) but which he manages to cede to the orchestra almost derisively, eight bars after it was their due.

Addressed to Leporello, the poem says, in a stanza-by-stanza précis: (1) Go prepare a party, (2) and bring some girls; (3) have them dance all kinds of uninhibited dances, (4) and I'll make love to many (5) and seduce/rape a dozen. (Da Ponte extended his four-line stanza deftly in stanza 3 to match the little dance inventory which recalls Leporello's equally cosmopolitan catalogue: 'Senza alcun ordine / la danza sia, / chi'l menuetto, / chi la folia, / chi l'allemana / farai ballar.') Whereas stanzas 1 and 4 are sung only once, making little impact, especially at the presto tempo, stanza 5 is repeated again and again, so that the message comes across four times in all, plus some fractions. What Giovanni actually says is 'you'll have to add *una decina* to my list'.

Mozart also repeats stanzas 2 and 3 – not, I think, because we have any further need to hear these particular words, but because he wants us to hear them with new, and newly ferocious, music. A single motif, very heavily accented, is barked out ten times near the top of the baritone's tessitura to accommodate the ten lines in these stanzas (and Giovanni's *decina*, no doubt):

2	*Se* trovi in *piazza*	(Girls in the piazza,
	*qual*che rag*azza,*	Girls in the market,
	*tec*o ancor *quel*la	Any you find there
	*cer*ca *men*ar . . .	Bring to the ball . . .

3	*Senza* alcun *ordine*	Set them to dancing,
	la danza *sia,*	All out of order:
	chi'l menu*etto,*	This one the high dance,
	chi la fo*lia,*	That one the low dance,
	chi l'alle*man*a	This one the mad dance,
	*far*ai bal*lar.*	We'll have them all.)

This is a musical procedure of unusual violence. The motif that recurs so blankly again and again is merely incantatory in melodic contour and obsessive in rhythm. Indeed the rhythm – starting with a dactyl: /.. / / – which dominates this little section dominates the aria as a whole; we are assailed by it in every one of the poem's twenty-two lines, starting with '*Fin* ch'han dal *vino*'. (By no means all of the lines take kindly to dactylic declamation.) In this section, the accents come twice as fast and hard as before.

'A crude expression of the phallic', or 'a feverish explosion of sheer sexual drive', according to some recent writers:[6] which is no doubt what earlier ones meant by the flesh incarnate or the life-force. However, Mozart had used fast driving rhythms of this kind before, in non-phallic contexts. He provided Figaro with such rhythms at the end of the minuet-like aria 'Se vuol ballare', when Figaro suddenly speeds up to spit out the words 'L'arte scher*mendo*, l'arte ado*prando*, / di qua pung*endo*, di la scher-*zando* . . .' (Subtly outwitting, innocent seeming, Cleverly hitting, planning and scheming). He provided Osmin with something similar, in anapaests, at the end of his big aria in *Die Entführung aus dem Serail*, when the goaded gaoler stutters his obscene, high-speed fantasy: 'Erst ge*köpft*, dann ge*hangen*, / dann ge*spiesst* auf heisse *Stangen*, / dann ver*brannt*, dann ge*bunden*, / und ge*taucht*, geletzt ge*schunden*' (First beheaded, then hanged, Then roasted on a hot griddle, etc.).

The situation in both of these earlier arias is similar. They begin with the characters expressing anger, but anger that has been brought under temporary control. Then they abruptly break down into explosions of uncontained fury (Figaro, unlike Osmin, ultimately regaining his self-control). 'Just as a man in such a towering rage oversteps all the bounds of order, so must the music too forget itself,' writes Mozart in a much-quoted letter about *Entführung*.[7] Rage is presented in stages. In 'Fin ch'han dal vino' the same *topos* – Monteverdi's *genere concitato* – is employed in isolation, without any warning; the special force, the menace of this aria comes from its projection of anger with precedent. This unmotivated anger (unmotivated by the dramatic action) is anger associated with, about, at, or in sex.

Jane Miller writes about an extended brutish trope in Richardson's *Clarissa* – where the brothel keeper Mrs Sinclair is described as a 'composite monster, dragon, hog, ferret and horse, distorted and curdled as it straddles and sputters'. Miller's words about this seem apropos here: 'The rape which is so bizarrely absent from the text itself has been displaced by the hatred it was intended both to express and discipline.'

How much angrier, by the way, 'Fin ch'han dal vino' seems than Masetto's aria 'Ho capito', in *Figarro*, where the singer is as funny as he is furious – distracted, confused, and tied up in knots by his aspirations to sarcasm.

V

To say that Don Giovanni's main aria is enraged may go some way towards explaining the aria's impact, but it does not do much to fill the void within the soul of No-Man. A negative quality of the piece also stands out, its lack of invention. At one point Giovanni boasts about his 'prolific talent' (*fertile talento*), but whatever talents he may possess, a talent for lyric fertility is not among them.

The 'Fin ch'han dal vino' jingle is just that, a jingle which never evolves. The melody never even forms into an antecedent–consequent pair, and when it comes back for the new words of stanza 5, it comes back unchanged. The music for the other stanzas does little more than thump, for the most part, and the cadencing, while unusually fierce, is as usual merely emphatic. Even one compensating rhythmic anomaly – the forceful cadential syncopation – is initiated by the orchestra, rather than by Giovanni's own invention.

It makes a critic uncomfortable, once again, to call a Mozart aria uninventive, let alone an entire Mozart role. Fortunately Mozart has left very many models of inventiveness in opera arias. One can try to compare 'Fin ch'han dal vino' in this respect with Cherubino's 'Non so più', Susanna's 'Venite inginocchiatevi', the Countess's 'Dove sono', Elvira's 'Mi tradì quell'alma ingrata', Tamino's 'Dies Bildnis ist bezaubernd schön', or the Queen of Night's 'Die Hölle Rache'. Some of these arias belong to Williams's 'self-reflective' category, others not. But in all of them, people keep thinking up new musical ideas and developing them prodigiously as a reflection of their own fertile emotional energies.

(*Così fan tutte* yields fewer such arias. Don Giovanni's artful second-act aria 'Metà di voi quà vadano' deserves a place in any such list; but while it may be diverting to speculate about a figure who can be creative only when disguised, presumably no one will be tempted to build a reading of Don Giovanni upon 'Metà di voi'. The key to his character cannot be found in a brilliant throwaway hidden in one of the plot's backwaters; it must be found in 'Fin ch'han dal vino', 'Là ci darem la mano', the Act I Introduction, the scene with the Commendatore – in the major scenes – or not at all.)

The Act I Introduction is another scene that does not show Giovanni in an inventive light. As remarked above, the scene does indeed present him with an unforgettable entrance, thanks to the stage action. But the music mutes this in a curious way which is not often remarked on, and which is worth pausing over for a moment. It seems Mozart and Da Ponte wanted explicitly to soft-pedal Giovanni's role in this episode.

This emerges with special clarity from the modelling situation. That Da Ponte copied much of the *Don Giovanni* libretto from a previous work, by Bertati, has already been mentioned. Set to music by Giuseppe Gazzaniga, an endlessly prolific but otherwise forgotten composer of the time, this opera held the stage for thirty years, playing in Paris and London as well as all over Italy.[8] Many of the scenes in *Don Giovanni* that we probably think of as among the most characteristic were modelled on Bertati: for example, the whole of the Act I Introduction, showing a grumbling man-servant who then comments on his master's struggle with a lady, a duel between the interloper and the lady's father, and the latter's death. Not the whole Introduction, but the episode with Anna is also a section of the opera where Mozart's music refers to Gazzaniga's (virtually the only such section). There are actual similarities of musical gesture.

Needless to say, in terms of musical detail the comparison is vastly to the advantage of Mozart; but this cannot be said so quickly of the comparison in terms of dramatic strategy. Mozart decided to play the scene for laughs, in effect – decided to play up Leporello's amused commentary on the action. Repeating himself much more than his opposite number in Gazzaniga, and in a much more unbuttoned fashion, the *buffo* bass ends up undercutting the struggle between the principals by nearly silencing them.

If Mozart bolstered Leporello's role, Da Ponte bolstered Anna's. Thus another difference from the Bertati–Gazzaniga opera is that Anna, not Giovanni, sings first. So the music Giovanni sings during their struggle is not of his own devising but echoed from Anna, as has often been observed. What is more, he also echoes her music later, when she has left, in the wonderful slow terzetto while he and Leporello watch the Commendatore die after the duel. (This terzetto, by the way, certainly does *not* have a precedent in Gazzaniga.) The dramatic point of Giovanni's low musical profile is clear enough in the first instance, when he is trying to hide his identity. What about the second?

The only reason I can think of for Mozart to have used old music here, in a situation where it would have been much more natural to use new, was to show Giovanni at a loss for words, for music. While Giovanni does not exactly regret the killing of the Commendatore, he is taken aback by its suddenness and unthinkingness; he might have wished for something else, if he ever took the trouble to think. Julian Rushton remarks with fine insight that Giovanni for once seems vulnerable. He is also revealed as lacking in musical, hence emotional, resource.

He is rather more resourceful in the wrenching scene with Donna Elvira in the second-act finale. Elvira bursts in on his dinner on the verge of breakdown, it seems – she can scarcely stay coherent long enough to beg him to save himself. Giovanni is at his most odious on this occasion, abandoning even the mask of civility. Towards the end of the scene, as he turns away from her with a blunt 'Lascia ch'io mangi' (leave me to my dinner), a piercing, mocking little tune emerges in the orchestra.

Giovanni has managed to generate music of his own; but the striking thing is that only half way through this tune does he think of words for it, a true afterthought – 'e se ti piace, mangia con me'.

(Inviting the humiliated Elvira to join him, at dinner or anything else, has to count as the acme of spontaneous cruelty.) The tune finally accommodates itself to Giovanni's tribute to women and good wine as the sustaining glory of mankind – 'Sostegno e gloria d'umanità'. Perhaps in concept it is a musical quotation of an actual toast, like the quotes from popular opera hits that we have just been hearing from the little *Tafelmusik* band.

The opera's seduction scenes, to be sure, resonate with Don Giovanni's music, music of his own invention. It is music that has been greatly and rightly admired. 'Là ci darem' gave Chopin the subject for variations with which to launch his career, and gave Peter Shaffer the centrepiece for one of the better scenes in *Amadeus* (the movie). Giovanni's serenade struck Charles Gounod – the composer of *Faust* – as 'a pearl of inspiration, alike in the elegance of its melody, harmony, and rhythm . . . a masterpiece of grace and gallantry' expressing 'an intensity of longing and marvellous captivation'. One cannot hear this music and doubt for a moment the deep truth (if not the statistical particulars) of Leporello's account of his master's success as a seducer.

Yet the actual lyric *development* of his music counts as very modest. I have already made the point that in 'Là ci darem' Giovanni issues the simplest of melodic units, and that it is Zerlina who invents the melody's adornments, extensions, diversions, and so on. In fact, Zerlina makes the piece her own. (She gets most of the opera's hit tunes.) As for Giovanni's later love-making, what is quite surprising about it is its repeated use of the same music. Giovanni sings approximately the same melody for his serenade to Elvira's maid, with strumming mandolin, as for his impromptu wooing of Elvira on behalf of the disguised Leporello. For all the difference of treatment, the similarity of melodic gesture is unmistakable.

There is a lesson here, no doubt, about the actual nature of improvisation. However this may be, we hear Giovanni fall back on a single formula, whether he finds himself in a formal situation or a spontaneous one. Why change, when success comes so automatically? Why invent?

When the Commendatore issues his fateful invitation to dinner, Don Giovanni answers with four bars of music:

Ho fermo il core in petto   (Stout-hearted,
Non ho timor. Verrò.   Unafraid: I'll come.)

To say that this music will probably not strike us as 'inventive' is not to deny its extraordinary impact (magnified by the awed response to it from the orchestra). These four bars could never have been predicted. Their unexpected features – stiff, pompous dotted rhythms and baroque-sounding counterpoint, provided by the strings alone – are also features of Donna Elvira's Act I aria 'Ah, fuggi il traditor', as Rushton has remarked:[9] one of those passing remarks that triggers (for me, at least) long unarticulated feelings about a work long known. They have nothing to do with Elvira, but everything to do with the antique quality of that strange aria of hers. Giovanni's language regresses to a hieratic mode of musical expression, as though to an archaic, frozen code of honour. Don Giovanni's finest moment is also, in a unique musical way, one of his most impersonal.

Perhaps it is labouring the obvious to say that what has been seen as a distinguishing feature of Don Giovanni since the time of Kierkegaard, namely his characterlessness, is compounded by uninventiveness. Bernard Williams, whose essay works to delimit idealistic accretions to Mozart's No-Man, none the less acknowledges Giovanni's sense of freedom and his recklessness, his

> single-minded determination to live life at the fullest energy, at the extreme edge of desire. . . . Those who survive Giovanni – not only the other characters, but, on each occasion that we have seen the opera, ourselves – are both more and less than he is: more, since, the conditions *on* humanity, which we accept, are also the conditions *of* humanity; and less, since one thing vitality needs is to keep the dream of being as free from conditions as his.[10]

Yet Giovanni was 'without love, compassion, and fairness, to mention only a few of the things he lacked'. Creativity was another of his chronic lacks. That is a big swatch of vitality to barter for a dream.

Notes

1 Bernard Williams, 'Don Juan as an idea', in Julian Rushton (ed.), *Don Giovanni* (Cambridge Opera Handbook; Cambridge, 1981), pp. 81–91; the quotations are on pp. 81 and 82.
2 Edward J. Dent, *Mozart's Operas* (London, 1913, 2nd edn., 1947), p. 185.
3 Wye Jamison Allanbrook, *Rhythmic gesture in Mozart: Le nozze di Figaro and Don Giovanni* (Chicago and London, 1983), p. 256.
4 See Daniel Heartz, 'Goldoni, Don Giovanni, and the dramma giocoso', *Musical Times* 120 (1979), pp. 993–8.
5 Williams, op. cit., p. 86.
6 John Stone, *Mozart-Jahrbuch 1984/85* (Cassell, 1986), p. 134; Charles Osborne, *The Complete operas of Mozart* (London, 1978), p. 268.
7 Emily Anderson (ed.), *Letters of Mozart and his family* (London, 1938), vol 3, p. 1144.
8 Giuseppe Gazzaniga, *Don Giovanni o sia Il convitato di pietra*, ed. S. Kunze (Cassell, 1974).
9 *Don Giovanni*, p. 107 (see note 1).
10 Williams, op. cit., pp. 90–91.

List of Contributors

JONATHAN MILLER is a doctor of medicine and director of many plays (including Beaumarchais's *The Marriage of Figaro* at the National Theatre) and operas (for English National Opera, Glyndebourne, Kent Opera, Australian Opera, Frankfurt, and Los Angeles, as well as BBC TV). He produced *Don Giovanni* for ENO in 1985. His account of his experiences as a producer, *Subsequent Performances*, is published by Faber (1986). He is Artistic Director of the Old Vic Theatre, London.

ROY PORTER is Senior Lecturer in the Social History of Medicine at the Wellcome Institute for the History of Medicine, London, and is the author of *English Society in the 18th Century* (1982), *The Anatomy of Madness*, 2 vols. (1985), co-editor (with G. B. Rousseau) of *Sexual Underworlds of the Enlightenment* (1987), and *Mind-Forged Manacles: Madness in 18th-Century England* (1987).

ROBERT DARNTON is Professor of History at Princeton University, USA, and the author of numerous eighteenth-century French studies including *The Great Cat Massacre* (1984), *The Business of the Enlightenment: A Publishing History of the Encyclopaedia, 1775–1800* (1979), *The Literary Underground of the Old Regime* (1982), and *Mesmerism and the End of the Enlightenment in France* (1968).

LAWRENCE LIPKING is Professor of English at Northwestern University, USA, and the author of *The Life of the Poet:*

Beginning and Ending Poetic Careers (1981), *Ordering of the Arts in 18th-Century England* (1970), and editor of *High Romantic Argument: essays for M. H. Abrams* (1981).

JANE MILLER teaches in the English and Media Studies Department of the University of London Institute of Education. She is author of *Many Voices: Bilingualism, Culture and Education* (1983), and *Women Writing About Men* (1986).

MALCOLM BAKER is Assistant Keeper in the Department of Sculpture at the Victoria and Albert Museum. He has written on various aspects of sculpture and the applied arts, particularly during the eighteenth century, and is currently working on a study of Roubiliac and the role of sculpture in mid-eighteenth-century England.

PETER GAY is Sterling Professor of History at Yale University, USA and has just completed a biography of Freud. He is the author of *The Enlightenment: an Interpretation*, 2 vols. (1966, 1969), *Education of the Senses* and *The Bourgeois Experience: from Victoria to Freud* (vol. 1, 1984; vol. 2, 1986).

PETER CONRAD is tutor in English at Christ Church, Oxford. His books include *Romantic Opera and Literary Form* (1977), and *The Everyman History of English Literature* (1985). His latest work is *A Song of Love and Death: The Meaning of Opera* (1987).

MARINA WARNER is the author of *Alone of All Her Sex: The Myth and the Cult of the Virgin Mary* (1976), *Monuments & Maidens: The Allegory of the Female Form* (1985), and, most recently, *The Lost Father*, a novel. In 1987–8 she was a Visiting Scholar at the Getty Center for the History of Art and the Humanities. She lives in London.

JOSEPH KERMAN is Professor of Music at the University of California at Berkeley, USA. The new edition of his *Opera as Drama* is published by Faber (1989); he is also the author of *Musicology* (1985), *The Masses and Motets of William Byrd* (1980), *The Beethoven Quartets* (1967), and a casebook on Mozart's Concerto in C Major, K.503.

Picture Credits

Grateful acknowledgment is made to the following for permission to reprint the plates appearing in this work:

P L A T E 1 : Monument to Bishop Francesco Morosini
© Osvaldo Böhm. Fotografo Editore, Riproduzioni D'arte, San Moise 1349-50, 30124 Venezia, Italy

P L A T E 2 : Monument to Wenzel, Count Wratislaw von Mitrowicz. Courtesy of Malcolm Baker

P L A T E 3 A : The corruption of the body
© Liberto Perugi Fotografo, 50124 Firenze, Via S Francesco di Paola 12, Italy

P L A T E 3 B : Two syphilitic figures
© Liberto Perugi Fotografo (address as given above)

P L A T E 4 : Monument to Arminius Maurice
© Courtauld Institute of Art. Conway Library, Courtauld Institute of Art, University of London, 20 Portman Square, London W1H OBE

P L A T E 5 : Monument to Daniel Gottlieb Mannlich
© Bildarchiv Foto Marburg

P L A T E 6 : Monument to Joseph Nightingale
© Dean and Chapter of Westminster. Courtesy of Dean and Chapter of Westminster

P L A T E 7 : Monument to Maria Magdalena Langhans
© Foatelier Gerhard Howald, Lindherain 7, Postfach CH-3038, Kirchenlineach-Bern, Switzerland

P L A T E 8 : Monument to Princess Charlotte
Reproduced by permission of the Dean and Canons of Windsor. The Treasurer to the Queen, The Royal Archives, Windsor Castle, Berkshire SL4 INJ